Talk to me, Baby

The Story of The Blues Band

by

Roy Bainton

Firebird Books

First published in the United Kingdom in 1994
by Firebird Books Ltd., P.O. Box 327,
Poole, Dorset BH15 2RG

Distributed in Australia by
Capricorn Link (Australia) Pty. Ltd.,
P.O. Box 6651, Baulkham Hills Business Centre, NSW 2153

A catalogue in publication data entry for this title is available from the British Library

ISBN 1 85314 201 8

Researched and designed by Allwrite Communications
Typeset by The TypeFoundry, Northampton
Monochrome Origination by Kilographics, London EC1
Printed and Bound in Great Britain by
Dorling Print Ltd., Mitcham

CONTENTS

This book is dedicated to my wife, Wendy.

Among the many, special thanks go to: Trevor Lewis, Phil Tyler, Doug Rose, Clive Truby, Geoff Evenden, Mike Reiach, Tony Corn, Chris Tigg, Chris Lloyd, Stuart and Katherine Booth, Dave Kelly and Gilly Tarrant for never letting me down, Rob for the open-ended day, Gary for being a good bloke, Tom and Paul for trusting me, Bob Brunning for being on the shelf should I need him, Peter for being a real gent, Hughie for inspiration, Bob and Hilary for being neighbours, Lari, Nicky and Des for keeping the show on the road .... and *you* – THE BLUES BAND FANS.

Thank You, Lonnie . . . .

I used to wonder what kind of a life my parents had before Rock & Roll. It seemed so odd that the backbeat, the excitement, the complete lifestyle we all began to indulge in after 1956 might not have been there before. The only exciting thing on British radio then between *Educating Archie* and *Ray's a Laugh* was the occasional Winifred Atwell record, a naughty snatch of that loose American, Glenn Miller, and La Compagnie du Chanson performing that perennial family favourite *Jimmy Brown*.

Whenever I see Judith Chalmers it always takes me back to the VBR; (Void Before Rock); a time of Meccano sets, the smell of sprouts boiling and cold blancmanges on a Sunday afternoon.

Of course, like some strange fourth dimension to which we war-weary British had no access, Rock & Roll was all around us; it crackled over hidden airwaves, was already rumbling across America and sneaking onto Merchant ships in the form of brash 78s. And there were those devoted aficionados who could foretell its arrival; they had been listening to something called 'The Blues' even before World War Two. Twelve bars and a bottleneck just prowled around, looking for a gang to join; the Blues had the Roll, boogie had the Rock. Before our elders could do anything about it the two had got together and that was the end of our pocket money. We went from being 'Young Ladies and Young Gents' overnight to something which had never previously existed; 'Teenagers'. To the generation who grew through this, the rest, as they say, is history. Those of you who came later might like to know what it was all like, not through the experiences of this two-bit scribe, but through the words of these fine musicians who took their enthusiasm beyond the queue in the record shop and up onto the stage.

During the last fourteen years I've interviewed Dave Kelly, his sister, the late Jo Ann, Bob Hall and others. One name cropped up every time we talked about the roots of British Blues. When I finally got around to talking in depth to Paul Jones and Tom McGuinness, I was taken aback when the same name moved centre-stage yet again. Who were they all queueing for in that mythical, pre-R&B record emporium? Who made it seem possible that you,

yes, you out there with the Brylcreem and the lumberjack shirt, you could make exciting music with a cheap guitar and a nasal twang? Lonnie Donegan, that's who.

Lonnie is something of a leitmotif throughout this book. He was of that pioneering generation ten years or more older than most of The Blues Band. Although he does not figure in any physical connection, like John Mayall, Alexis Korner or Cyril Davies in the following chapters, all of us who love our Blues and Rock, those who lift their pewter tankards with pride at the weekly Folk Club, every would-be Lester Flatt or Earl Scruggs is in debt to Donegan. Unlike most of the Blues Band, I did actually meet the King of Skiffle. At the time he was riding high in the charts with *Puttin' on the Style*. It was in the Autumn of 1957 and I stood in the electric darkness outside the stage door of the Regal in Hull's bus station. In those days bands played two houses; between the first set, which finished about 8.15, and the second house, the stars, if brave enough, might even nip out to a local hostelry for refreshments. At the Regal in Hull they were blessed with the White Lion, only seconds away from the stage door. First to return from the pub were the charming, accommodating Donegan band members, bassist Micky Ashman and drummer Nick Nicholls. No trouble with autographs and pats on the young teenager's back there. It began to drizzle. With only minutes to spare before his appearance, the Skifflemeister, wearing a Burberry fit for a Bogart, sauntered towards the stage door. My heart leapt. I thrust forward the autograph book, opened my mouth to tell him how thrilling his music was, but a wiry, Burberried arm thrust me aside. "Piss off, kid! Can't you see it's fuckin' rainin'?"

If you're out there, Lonnie, I forgive you, but I would still like your autograph, just for old time's sake....

Almost a quarter century later, in the midst of a burgeoning electro-music scene and the tail-end of Punk, we discovered a band playing good, honest R&B in a style we'd long since given up as dead. To be honest, without the open, organic thrust of the Punk phenomenon the Blues Band may well have had a harder time. It was the raw, irreverent energy of the Pistols, The Clash and The Damned which flushed out the flaccid S-bend of so-called 'progressive' rock, with it's boringly long solos and pretentious, vacuous lyrics. Punk took the concept album into the car-park and gave it a good kicking, and music was all the better for it.

Of course, there were other people playing R&B during that period. It would be folly to overlook the contribution of bands like Dr. Feelgood, Nine Below Zero and Lew Lewis, all of whom created that vital atmosphere in the London pubs in the late '70s, where a blues hungry and frustrated actor called Jones became a regular fixture, trying to figure out how he was going to get back to the music he loved, when, where and with whom.

Pop music, after the 1950s, became a 'generation' thing. If you played pop, you had to be young. The post war teenage market was a vast money-mine for the record industry. Before the war, music was music. Henry Hall and Roy Fox played dance band music, and you could neither tell nor care what age they were. The 'Teenage' phenomenon changed all that. Youth was everything, and the music press moved away from serious comment and criticism to a flippant disregard for anything outside the charts. To some extent, that attitude has continued. You could well be over fifty and sit at your computer, make a mega club-mix rave record, press it up and, if the DJs like it, you can have a hit. But if you want to put it on *Top of The Pops*, you'd better hire three Lycra-clad youngsters to act it out. You'll not go far with a balding pate and a beer belly.

There are lots of reasons why The Blues Band, as opposed to any blues band, became and remain a success. Many middle-agers with some disposable income just love the 'train-spotting' aspect of col-

lecting Blues records. Paul Jones and Bob Hall, for instance, relish their knowledge of matrix numbers, alternative takes and inside-leg measurements. The difference for Blues Band Fans is, to some degree, to do with pedigree.

Unlike the the younger bands, high on energy and enthusiasm though they are, The Blues Band represent a living enclave of Transatlantic Pop Heritage. They were there; they built the original machines. They are a kind of working tram museum or steam railway, and we fans lovingly polish and preserve them.

The Blues Band didn't do just what the critics might have expected them to do. As musicians with plenty of creative ability they could well have opted for the rambling solo and the mutual instrumental jazzman's pat-on-the-back. It was their long experience of Rock'n'Roll showmanship which kept all that at bay. Here was blues you could handle. Blues in neat, frantic parcels. Numbers just long enough for an audience which had been weaned on the 2-minute Chuck Berry single or the five minute Bo Diddley bash. Thoughtful arrangements, compact, showcase solos; a touch of glamour and a sense of humour. The Blues Band have something for the women, plenty for the men, and a cracking ability to write modern songs in the R&B idiom. All this makes for a unique configuration, still being discovered by both young and old. Blues Band fans know what they've got; not something huge and unapproachable; if U2 are a jumbo jet, then the Blues Band are a trusty old Dakota. In 1992 they toured Europe, playing support to Dire Straits. Their audiences reached 40,000 per night. A long way from The Bridge House pub in April 1979. They were the right band for the right job. Their job is playing the Blues, and no European band does it better.

Some of today's Blues Band audiences may have found Punk puzzling and distasteful, but when a drain needs unblocking, then hell, somebody has to do it. So it's not only Lonnie, but Johnny, we have to thank, no matter how rotten he made you feel. It is worth remembering that Punk was all about raw self-expression which is, when you come down to it, the very essence of the Blues.

"Can You Play Simply?"

The Tom McGuinness Story

Tom McGuinness was born in Wimbledon in 1941. His father was a builder's labourer from County Longford in Ireland, and his mother came from County Cork. His father moved to England in the 1920s, and his mother in the 1930s. They met, got married.

"As far as I'm concerned", says Tom, "I'm Irish. When Ireland play England at football I don't have any doubts about that. I know most people would think of Wimbledon as the home of tennis and very posh, but in the part I was born in and grew up in everyone was Irish. I went to the Catholic Primary School and everyone was called McGuinness, O'Brien or McCarthy. And when I went to the Grammar School it was predominantly Irish. We went to Ireland for our holidays. One thing I don't understand is why I'm an only child; my father came from a family of twelve brothers and sisters and my mother came from a family of twelve brothers and sisters. They were hard workers. My father didn't retire until he was 70, and he only retired then because they told him he had to go. Even then he got a job in a supermarket stacking the shelves and he was supposed to make sure that people weren't shoplifting, but he was hopeless at that bit. He never had the heart to report anyone he saw shoplifting because he felt sorry for them. Then he went to work in a furniture warehouse part time. I remember him saying then that most of his workmates who'd retired at 65 were dead. But he kept active. Sadly, he died in 1984. He'd moved back to Ireland two years before, and my mother passed away in 1975.

"I left school not knowing what I wanted to do and not really qualified to do anything. I ended up working for the Norwich Union's Insurance office. After two years I realised that this was going to drive me mad, or into an early grave. What I really wanted to do was write. Looking back, I find that insurance job unbelievable; I actually passed insurance exams, but I tend to be one of those people who, if they have to do something, think 'Well, I'm going to try and do it well....' but eventually it got to me.

However, I'd never thought about being a professional musician then. This was mainly due to the fact that what I really wanted to play was rhythm and blues, and there was no market for that kind of music. This was at the beginning of 1963, just after I'd given up the office job. What I was trying to do was write; humourous pieces and The Great British Screenplay. No, there wasn't 'The Novel' but I did have a breakthrough with one piece on *That Was The Week That Was*. I was writing that material with an old schoolfriend called Mark Newell. Together we set about bombarding *Private Eye* and *TW3* and similar outlets.

"Unfortunately, the *TW3* piece was the only success; my money ran out and I had to take a job as a furniture porter. I'd got nearly nine months out of my pension contribution at the Norwich Union which I got back from them when I left. It was good, but it didn't last. Fortunately I was still living at home. The porter's job was at Bentalls in Kingston. Bentalls at the time was like an adjunct of the DHSS. It was filled with unemployed musicians and actors, who were all.... 'resting', so they'd go and work for Bentalls for a few weeks. When I arrived there, I immediately thought 'this will also drive me mad....'

"During this period in 1963, I had got a band together – The Roosters. The line-up included Eric Clapton. I'd been introduced to Eric by my girlfriend, Jennifer Dolan, who was at Kingston College of Art with him. Ben Palmer played piano, and an old schoolfriend, Terry Brennan, sang and played harmonica. On drums we had Robin Mason, who I have never heard of since. It was difficult then to find musicians. We never had a bass player. It seems surprising today, but at the time there weren't many people who wanted to actually play in a rhythm and

Pre-everything – Tom with The Talismen, very early '60s

blues band. You really felt as if it was a branch of Freemasonry.

"The band only lasted until September and it fell apart. Then Eric and I went off to join Casey Jones and the Engineers. We were only in there for about six weeks; it was also driving us mad simply because Casey Jones couldn't sing. We had to play *Poison Ivy* and *I'm a Hog for You Baby*, songs like that, whilst he leapt around looking charming. I suppose he was a kind of prototype Herman, but without the talent. I continued to work as a furniture porter, but during this period I'd been in regular contact with Paul Jones. The Roosters had played support to Manfred's band at the Marquee and we'd had this big argument with Manfred because we weren't getting enough money. He said 'But everyone plays for that money as a support act', but we said 'Well – it's not enough!' His reply was simple; 'Well – don't do it, then!'

"However, I stayed in touch with Paul. I knew they were unhappy with their bass player. I then actually lied to Paul, saying 'Guess what – I'm playing bass these days....'

"I met Paul through an advert in the *Melody Maker*. Ben Palmer was advertising for blues musicians

in 1962. His advert was on the lines 'I would like to join a band playing the music of Muddy Waters, Elmore James and Sonny Boy Williamson'. I replied saying 'Yes! I too would like to join a band playing that music – if you find such a band, will you tell me!' Ben and I then got together. He was a friend of Paul. They had a band together in Oxford. I not only met Paul through Ben Palmer; I also met my first wife, too; she was Ben's sister-in-law. This was after Paul had been sent down from Oxford University. I went over to Oxford for a weekend and we all chatted. We tried hard to find a drummer, a bass player, failing miserably. People just didn't turn up for auditions or rehearsals. But Paul and I stayed in touch. We weren't on the phone then, but I remember getting a letter from Paul. As I said earlier, I'd lied about my bass-playing. The letter said: 'Come to the St. John's Ambulance Hall, Chigwell, Essex, on Friday night.... and you may learn something to your advantage....'

"When I arrived there, the founder members of The Mann-Hugg Blues Brothers, Manfred and Mike Hugg, took me off into one room while Mike Vickers took Dave Richmond, the then bass player, off into another. My audition consisted of being asked the question: 'Will you promise to play.... simply?' Dave Richmond was a really great bass player, but he was like Charlie Mingus – he would fly off at a tangent all the time because I think he found playing rhythm and blues boring, being a jazz musician. Now, I could say, with my hand on my heart that I would play 'simply', because I'd never touched a bass guitar in my life. Fortunately I didn't have to play that Friday night. I trekked off home from Chigwell to Twickenham. By this time I was living with Ruth, who became my first wife, and she was pregnant. If you look at the tube map, you'll see that it's a long, long way from Chigwell to Richmond. I just left the Mann-Hugg Blues Brothers at their gig. When I got home, Ruth asked me what I thought. I said they'd never be able to make up their minds; there seemed to be a lot of 'umming and arring'. The next morning I stumbled out of bed and went off to moving the furniture at Bentalls. Ruth rang me there later in the day. 'Did you see the note'? My reply was 'What note'? Apparently they'd called round at four in the morning and pushed this note through the door saying 'You've got the job – be at The Ealing Club tonight at seven.' When I arrived home that night, I went out with Ruth and a friend of hers for a drink. I looked at my watch and it was half past six. Suddenly I realised my watch had stopped. This was to be my big night and Ruth then informed me it was ten to seven and I'd miles to travel! However, I got there just in time for the gig, was handed a bass guitar, and, as requested, and due to this being the first bass I had ever picked up, played.... very simply. Probably too simply, in fact, because they were still playing quite a lot of jazz stuff at this time. The line up was Mike Vickers on guitar, saxophone and flute, Manfred on Keyboards, Paul on vocals and harmonica, Mike Hugg on drums and me on bass. They were doing Chuck Berry and Bo Diddley numbers as well as stuff from Cannonball Adderley. It was quite a mixture. We even used to do a Miles Davis tune.

"I remember those first few gigs for one particular reason. I arrived at that first gig and thought, 'Hey – this is brilliant! You don't even have to set up your own equipment....'

"For the next four nights, I turned up just about five minutes before we were due to go on stage until one night, Paul took me discreetly to one side and whispered "Would you mind arriving at the same time as the rest of us and helping us to set the equipment up?" Up until then it hadn't crossed my mind; I thought it just appeared on stage as if by magic!

"By the time I joined Manfred the band had already recorded three singles. They'd released *Why Should We Not* and *Cock-a-Hoop* and they'd already recorded *54321*. I'd joined in December '63; I think it was about the 22nd, so the bass playing on those records isn't me – that's Dave Richmond. Come February and *54321* was a huge hit. Looking back, I was lucky to have joined the band simply on Paul's recommendation; they'd been slogging around the country for a whole year, building up a tremendous following, I walked into the band and they immediately have a hit record.

"They'd built up such a devoted following. They did the Marquee on a Monday night, Portsmouth on Tuesdays, Southampton Wednesday, Bournemouth on Thursdays, The Ealing Club on Saturday, and every gig was packed out.

"When I'd been working at Norwich Union, I'd been earning about five pounds a week. At Bentalls it was probably seven or eight pounds. Suddenly, after joining Manfred, here I was earning fifteen pounds a week. Now that was a lot of money in those days.

McGuinness and Culture – never far apart

9

The Roosters, 1963, with fledgling Eric Clapton, left

"In a very short time this went up to fifty pounds a week – cash!

"I always had a pile of money on the mantelpiece. I used to look at it and realise I just didn't know what to do with it. I was so busy. I didn't even have a proper stereo unit. I mean, even after we'd had eight hit records I couldn't play any of them; I had this Dansette sitting in the middle of the room, but there was simply no time; no time to play records, no time to spend my money. It was a great time. I remember just after joining the band I returned to Bentalls. I'd actually called in after the Christmas break for my cards and my wages. It was about ten in the morning on about 8th January and there was the foreman saying 'It's no good you coming back now'. I told him I'd come for my cards and that I'd joined a band. He shook his head in dismay, saying 'Ha! You'll not get anywhere doing that!' I replied 'Well.... you could be right, but just watch the television, Friday night, six o'clock – I'm on!'

"And that was *Ready, Steady, Go!* and we were previewing *54321* which had actually been commis-sioned as the theme tune. I just remember the joy of telling that foreman that I was on television.

ENTER HUGHIE

"As time rolled on we were working quite a lot. Just being in a rhythm and blues band meant that we met lots of other blues players; we were in and out of each other's gigs, meeting up on motorways, sitting in with each other's bands.

"I can't actually pinpoint when I met Hughie Flint. I remember sitting in with John Mayall's Bluesbreakers and of course, Hughie was there. By this time I'd married Ruth, my first wife, and Ben Palmer had separated from Jo, who was Ruth's sister, and Hughie started going out with Jo. So there was this kind of family connection going on; John Mayall lived just down the road from us in Lee Green, Hughie lived not far away in Blackheath.

"Towards the end of The Manfreds, Hughie wasn't playing with anyone and I thought it seemed it was such a waste of his talent, so he would come along and play percussion with the Manfreds;

congas and such. Then the Manfreds broke up.

"First of all, I thought I wasn't going to do anything."

"I thought well.... you don't get a 'second chance' at music. I took a whole summer off from music. Throughout the sixties everything had been so hit singles-based. The constant theme was 'You're only as big as your last hit....' and when it suddenly stopped, I spent the whole summer going to art galleries and museums and doing all those things I'd never had time to do when the band had been touring so much. Then one fine day, Hughie and I were sitting quietly in the pub and we had a conversation along the lines of 'Aren't The Band great – why don't we form a band like The Band?'

"And that's how McGuinness Flint came into being.

"Other interconnected things were happening at that time. At the very end of the sixties, together with Gerry Bron, the Manfred's manager, I had set up a company making what we today call pop videos; we called them 'promos' then. An old friend of mine, Luke Kelly (no relation to Dave and not the

Hughie, sans beard, early '70s

Luke Kelly of the Dubliners!), was also involved. Tony Scott was the director – he went on to make *Top Gun* – we made a promo for Colosseum, among others. It was Tony Reeves of Colosseum who told Hughie and I about two great Scots singer-songwriters. They could play as well, apparently. So, I gave them a ring and they came along and it all fell together; McGuinness Flint had a line-up. The two Scots, of course, were Benny Gallagher and Graham Lyle; Benny, myself and Graham all swapped instruments in the band, alternating between bass, mandolin, guitar and banjo. Hughie was on drums, and we had a singer, Dennis Coulson, who we'd found before Gallagher & Lyle. He sang a lot on McGuinness Flint albums too; sang lead, but Graham Lyle sang the lead on our two hit singles. Dennis made one album for Elektra after that and then vanished.... into tree pruning.

"Eventually, McGuinness Flint finished. Graham and Benny left in – I think it was '71 – really because they weren't enjoying it. They weren't enjoying the live performing. We didn't do that many gigs partly because we simply hadn't found the right way to do it. We couldn't present ourselves very well. It was still a good band, mind you; apart from our success here *When I'm Dead and Gone* made number thirty in the U. S. charts, which was pretty good going. But I was a bit shell shocked by their leaving. I didn't want to get another band together, but we were bored.

"I made an anti-internment record with McGuinness Flint which was banned. I'd put this huge band together to play the Empire Pool, Wembley – the first time I'd ever sung lead on stage – this record had come out and got a lot of play. It was a Worker's Revolutionary Party or Socialist Worker's gig. Paul was there, Slade were there, Hughie played drums, Mickey Waller played drums, we had about three saxophone players, ten people singing backing vocals, Dixie Dean on bass. It was quite an occasion.

"Eventually, Hughie and myself, Dixie Dean, and Dennis Coulson, we all went into the studio and made an album of Bob Dylan songs called *Lo and Behold*, which came out to incredible critical acclaim. *Rolling Stone* said that it was the best Dylan album since *Blonde on Blonde*, and as a result of that, we were approached to reform McGuinness Flint. So, we got a Canadian pedal steel player in

Hair today – a furry Tom McGuinness in McGuinness Flint days

called Jim Evans. We were still totally into The Band, as well as a couple of Grateful Dead albums, *Working Man's Dead* and *American Beauty*.

"We were also quite enjoying the whole pub rock scene then with bands like Brinsley Schwarz and Bees Make Honey. McGuinness Flint '2' was a much better live band, but without Benny and Graham, the material wasn't as good. Lou Stonebridge joined us on keyboards, guitar and harmonica. He'd come from a band called Paladin; they were a 'progressive' rock outfit. Before that he was in Glass Menagerie. He was experienced in the studio because both those bands had done quite a bit of recording. Lou had been recommended to us by one of the Manfred Mann's Earthband road crew. It was funny; whenever we auditioned people for McGuinness Flint, it didn't seem to have results, but when someone said 'why don't you try so-and-so' they invariably fitted in; it worked; just as it had when Paul recommended me for Manfred; they could have probably auditioned twenty bass players; without any undue big-headedness it was perhaps that I just brought something of my own to the

band, and that's how it seemed to work when people were recommended to us.

"McGuinness Flint '2' had quite a good run until in 1975 Hughie was quite ill and went into hospital with a collapsed lung. It seemed as good a time as any to pack things in. We'd recorded two albums for Bronze. Lou and I had been writing together quite a lot during this period. When the band broke up, Bronze offered us a songwriting contract. That kept us going for a couple of years. We wrote a lot of material, had a hit record in France with Sylvie Vartan which earned thousands, and a song I'd written for McGuinness Flint called 'C'est La Vie' was a big hit in Germany for a German band, so the money kept on rolling in.

"Lou and I were producing a little bit and then we were offered a recording deal by RCA and recorded an album; *Stonebridge McGuinness*. This would be '78–'79. We also made a couple of singles as Stonebridge McGuinness, one of which reached number one in the *Time Out* critics chart even though it only sold about three. In fact, we were recording the Stonebridge McGuinness album for RCA in the spring and summer of '79 and the Blues Band had already been formed while that was going on. Lou was even asked to join the Blues Band at one point.

"At the time The Blues Band was formed the only live work Lou and I were doing was the occasional gig with two guitars in wine bars, simply to 'keep our hand in'. We had a decent living coming in from various sources; the odd royalty, plus the fact that publishers would sign Lou and I to various songwriting deals. We signed with a new company called Heath Levy – we were with them for three years – they paid us an advance at the start of each year. We were doing lots of things and our living was music. There was production, too; I produced an album with Brewer's Droop.

"And then; The Blues Band. I recall Paul giving me a call one night. He was missing the blues and fancied putting a couple of gigs together. He came over, we discussed the material and I was keen on the idea. Paul asked if I could think of anyone else to ask. When McGuinness Flint had folded, Hughie had taken a job as a postman. I thought he might fancy the idea. He did, providing there was just the odd gig and no major commitment. I had a very good friend, a banjo player called Keith Nelson. He said 'Guess who delivered my laundry today – Dave Kelly'. We rang Dave; he said yes. He knew Gary Fletcher, who was driving a minicab at the time. He told us that Gary played bass so I said 'bring him along!'

"At that first rehearsal Dave didn't even realise who the harp player was at first. He said 'Isn't that the bloke from Manfred Mann?' But none of that mattered; we'd just got together to play some blues. However, we didn't want to fall into the rut of long, self indulgent solos. It was to be tight arrangements, varied numbers which would make for an entertaining show. And that was part of the reason why we were a success. We were never boring.

"The first gig, in April 1979 at The Bridge House, took us totally by surprise. You couldn't park a car within three quarters of a mile from the pub. We didn't realise until we finally got there that they were all there for us. The place was packed. During those first months we made various live recordings at gigs, but there was no actual record. We had a couple of tracks on the Albion Label compilation, *The London R&B Sessions*, recorded at The Hope & Anchor. But at that time we didn't have any firm plans about being 'professional'. We'd done a couple of gigs and people kept throwing offers at us, you know, will you do The Half Moon, the Hope & Anchor – all around the London area.

"Suddenly there was a real buzz going around. Ron Watts, who had been the lead singer in Brewer's Droop and around on the Blues scene for years with The National Blues Federation – they used to bring artists over for gigs – Ron ran a gig at The Nag's Head in High Wycombe. He'd booked The Blues Band for September 1979 and off we all went in our little cars; me in my Morris Traveller, Paul in his little Renault, I can't remember what the others were driving. Anyway, we all arrived at The Nag's Head about 5.30 on this beautiful late summer's evening and Ron turned up and said 'What're you lot doin' 'ere?' We said 'Ron.... you've booked us to appear!' He said 'No I haven't!' I think he'd rung Dave or one of us two months before. He said 'Naw! I've got the Merton Parkas tonight – a Mod revival band – they'll draw a bigger crowd than you. I'm sorry, lads. I don't remember booking you. Here's a tenner – go away!'

"So there we were, sat in the bar. It was at this point we realised that we had to become professional.

We needed someone to look after us; we had to make a record, because people were asking for one. We agreed that we needed a manager; so we said.... 'Who?' I suggested Ray Williams, who had until then been managing Lou Stonebridge and myself. So we all went up and met Ray. But Ray certainly didn't find it easy to find us a record deal. However, he did come up with some good ideas – like doing it ourselves. And that's how *The Bootleg Album* came about. We had this stuff in the can, and Ray knew the people who ran the Our Price record chain. They said they'd take a thousand albums if we pressed them up ourselves, so as we seemed to be nowhere near being offered a deal by anyone, that's just what we did. Before we knew it, we'd delivered thousands of albums and we made the Our Price best sellers chart. Now that just tied in with the Midem Festival in Cannes. Ray went down there and said 'Look – this album has sold over five thousand in just a week – it's in the Our Price charts and it's available.' Arista did a deal there and then to take it over. It sold tens of thousands and still sells well today – it's one of the most popular with the fans."

Mike McGear (McCartney) and Tom

"It all comes round again. In '82, when the Band played what we thought was our final gig at The Venue in Victoria, London, it all seemed so black and white. Hughie had left the year before and it wasn't surprising; he didn't want the pressure. Paul was having great difficulty fitting in his various theatre commitments. We'd reached a stage where we were unable to deal with each other's needs. With Paul's commitment to The National Theatre, we felt it was them or us. No-one considered the possibility of putting the band on ice for a while, working occasionally.... no. We just thought 'That's it!'

"Yet here we are. I just love playing. I cannot understand how anyone can just stop playing; Hughie, for instance. I know he's happy now but.... how can you just stop, like that?"

And the future?

"I hope I'll go on playing until I drop.... that's my intention...."

Tom McGuinness's career in music has been a seamless journey, full of interlocking turns of good fortune, meetings at the right time with the right people. It may well be that talent recognises talent, but none of the break-ups of various projects had too disastrous an effect as there were always new and challenging opportunities waiting just around the corner. There was his book, the highly-amusing So You Want to be a Rock & Roll Star; his TV work, which produced the wonderful South Bank Hendrix biography. And even the first break up of the Blues Band wasn't the trauma it may have been. Like any good craftsman knows, once you've built one house, there's always another to work on.

Tom swaps picks with B.B. King

Grits ain't Groceries

The Dave Kelly Story

We'll avoid all the clichés about the 'South London Delta'. Dave Kelly was born in Streatham in 1947. His father was like his son; he could turn his hand to anything. In many ways, what you hear in Dave Kelly's blues is just about as natural as the music can get considering the man is neither black or American. His sister, the late, great Jo Ann Kelly, was ahead of him in those early days in Streatham, but little brother Dave soon caught up. Dave is no blues 'anorak'; unlike many of his contemporaries he doesn't collect matrix numbers and his days of searching for long-lost recordings of Louisiana field hollers are long past.

Dave Kelly is a craftsman who served an enviable apprenticeship. He toured with Howlin' Wolf and John Lee Hooker, both of whom became friends to their young English sideman. In New York he jammed with Muddy Waters,, Hubert Sumlin, Walter Horton and Otis Spann. He's appeared on TV with Buddy Guy, and has played in countless classic UK blues line-ups over the past three decades. It may have brought fame, but his fortune still lies in his organisational ability and impressive, down-home versatility. Plumbing, electrical wiring, plastering, cab driving, delivering laundry – here's your man. And an accomplished chef to boot. These days, between playing and endless travelling you're more likely to find DK behind his Agent's desk, hotly pursuing by fax and phone the next deal for The Blues Band. Not a man to suffer fools gladly, Dave Kelly is, simply, the business.

"It was rock'n'roll which started it for me. My parents had some Western Swing records; I remember being about nine or ten and hearing *Smoke That Cigarette*. I was already playing guitar as rock broke onto the scene. I remember my first guitar. It was a 4-string acoustic, cost about eleven pounds. I did learn piano properly and I had lessons, although I don't play now. I also got into the trombone at the same time – it was great fun, and I wouldn't mind playing it again. My idols in those days were Lonnie Donegan, Elvis, Little Richard and especially Buddy Holly. Holly was so uncomplicated but so good; I particularly remember the guitar break on *Looking For Someone to Love*; great stuff.

"There used to be a great record shop in Streatham – Carey's Swing Shop. Jo Ann was always in there, because unlike any other shop we knew of at the time they were importing blues records. All I knew was that it was certainly different to skiffle and had immense appeal. I'd begun playing folk music; traditional English, Scottish and Irish material. But then I heard Leadbelly and Big Bill Broonzy, and through Jo Ann I met Tony McPhee, who went on to form The Groundhogs. The Rolling Stones had started playing their Sunday afternoon sessions at Studio 51. That's when I saw a slide guitar being played – Brian Jones. I was around seventeen when I first heard Robert Johnson. It was a decisive moment – I knew what I wanted to do.

"I met John Lee Hooker through Tony McPhee, who had backed him on his trips over here. Hooker told me that if ever I was in the States I should call him. When I arrived in New York I went to meet him at the theatre. Just imagine what it was like; eighteen years old, going backstage with John Lee Hooker to be introduced to his friend, Muddy Waters. I went into the dressing room and there was a line-up of legends; Otis Spann, Hubert Sumlin and Big Walter Horton. After I'd spoke with Muddy for a while, I asked him if I could play his guitar. I started playing and he said 'Hey, man, you can really play that thing!' There was laughter all round, everyone plugged in and before we knew it we were jamming. I suppose they were surprised; it was 1966 and here was a white kid, from England, playing country blues. Hooker was laughing at Muddy and saying 'Yeah, man – this boy's got all your shit off!' It was a great time.

Dave (right) with the John Dummer Band circa 1968

"When I got back to England I got a call from Bob Hall. I'd met Bob in about 1963 when he was playing piano with Jo Ann in jazz clubs. In those days, of course, Bob Hall was a lot older than me. Anyway, Bob asked me if I'd like to join a band. The line up was Tony Walker, bass, Steve Rye on harmonica and John Dummer on drums. I suddenly realised there was some work to be done. For instance, I didn't even have a pick-up on my guitar; I got Tony McPhee to help me out there. I practised by playing along to records by Buddy Guy, Muddy and Junior Wells. I particularly liked Elmore James. We rehearsed and I really enjoyed it. Tony Walker didn't seem too interested in the band, so we decided to lose him because we'd heard a rumour that our bass-player-to-be, Iain 'Thumper' Thompson, had a van. Well, we got Thump, but we found out the van was just that – a rumour.

"At this time just about every record company was signing blues bands. We got a deal with Mercury. I always thought we needed a proper lead guitarist, and as McPhee wasn't doing much, I asked him if he'd like to come in, and he agreed. It was a very good band, and the album we made, *Cabal*, still stands up today. I note with some disgust that it's out

on CD as a bootleg – some Dutch outfit has issued it.

"We were on the road, had management, an agency. It was up and down the motorway, then Europe. There was a lot of dope going around at the time, too, and I got a bit paranoid. We made a couple of albums, but eventually I got fed up with the company of the Dummer Band; not because they were nasty blokes or anything like that, it's just the old story of living in each other's pockets for too long. I remember arriving back after a Scandinavian tour, looking forward to a two week holiday only to find the two weeks had been filled with ten gigs. I just said 'No way – I'm off'. Our manager had the third album in mind and he'd already booked studio time. He said 'Can you just go in and record something?' Well... I went in and did about three or four tracks but the atmosphere was a bit strained; working with people you'd just left because you couldn't get on with them; it was all a bit stupid. After all that I looked for something new and formed a band called Rock Salt. As luck would have it, the Dummer Band went on, without me, to have a million seller in France. I'd suggested they got Nick Pickett in to replace me. Nick was a violinist as well as a guitarist and he wrote this instrumental called *Nine by Nine*; Stephane Grapelli covered it and it made a lot of money – for Nick's manager! I don't think Nick saw any of it. I did some solo stuff then, and a solo album for Mercury – just called *Dave Kelly*. It was crap, but unfortunately it keeps turning up here and there and I attempt to buy them all and turn them into fruit bowls. There's some nice songs on there but I had no sense of direction and I didn't know what I was doing. I was just concerned with getting out of the recording contract. My manager at the time was keen to get me to sign up with one of Pye's psychedelic offshoot labels – all very acid. I didn't realise that Peter Eden wanted me to sign and I think I probably offended him. He'd even employed Laurence Myers, who is now one of the top Music Biz lawyers, to get me out of the contract. I just didn't understand the situation and I told Peter Eden I'd do the Pye thing some time in the future. Needless to say I didn't. He runs a music shop now in Southend. I was very naive about the business then and in a way I wanted to remain so.

"Rock Salt was a very good live band. Our recordings were a bit boring, but it was a good line-up, with Keith Nelson on banjo, Cedric Thorose on mandolin and fiddle, Thump on bass and an Australian, who's still over here, Peter Miles, on drums, Adrian Pietryga on guitar. As I said, I'd left the Dummer Band when they had the French million-seller, and although the band had ceased working, the French record company asked if we could take 'a John Dummer Band' across there. So we took Rock Salt across and the French were very impressed; the press would come up to us and say 'But we thought you were a "pop" band', and they loved what we did. We were playing an interesting mix of music at the time; it was like electric bluegrass, very bluesy and country, quite before its time in many ways. Then Phonogram wanted another Dummer Band album and that was the end of Rock Salt. This new Dummer line-up was the Ooblee Dooblee Band. We cut the album then the line-up expanded with Pete Emery joining us on guitar and Colin Earl on piano, who went off to join Mungo Jerry. Our second album was unissued; we had no agent and the whole thing petered out. We had a guy called Pete Richardson on half that album on drums because Dummer had left. Pete was very young, not a bad drummer. His brother ran The

Rubettes, and that was his claim to fame. He left and got married, so Pick Withers joined us, who, as you know, went on to join Dire Straits.

"By 1974 The Ooblee Dooblee Band, after two albums, broke up. My son, Sam, was born. I took a day job, delivering laundry, but I kept on playing. We formed a pub band called Dogs. Thump was still with us, and Wilgar Campbell, Rory Gallagher's drummer. We advertised for a guitar player and got George Currie, who was pretty good. The Dogs were a pub band, we played what I'd describe as 'acid blues'. We played a couple of years and we recorded virtually every night. A friend of ours had a Revox tape deck. He was a theatre sound engineer and he would often bring this huge 32-channel desk out of the theatre, set it up in the back of the pub and record the set. He must have recorded over thirty gigs. I've still got the tapes; God knows what they must sound like. Even the short numbers were twenty minutes long. I got tired of delivering laundry and took a job at Smithfield Market delivering

Dave with son, Sam.

meat. It was my most vegetarian period ever. Not just because it was so revolting, handling meat; I'd spent nearly a year as a vegetarian cook in an enterprise run by a friend and my wife's sister. (I've lost track of the chronology here) – but that meat really went against the grain. I was still gigging regularly, but after the Dogs split, Thump went into a band called The Jive Bombers, which was Jonah Lewie on keyboards, Martin Stone on guitar, Will Stallybrass on harmonica. Nothing happened, but eventually all that evolved into Darts.

"So there's me, driving a laundry van again, watching all my old mates shoot up the charts. I went back to the Folk Clubs and solo recording. I hit a period of depression; if you want it warts and all, it was clinical depression and I had treatment for it. I had a long period of saying 'no' to everything. I didn't want to play, do anything. Then I began to say 'yes'. I was approached by the South London Theatre Group, which was a fairly professional amateur group. They asked me to write the music and perform in a play, *The Sport of My Mad Mother*. It

was a hard decision, but I was just beginning to turn a corner so I went for it. It turned out very well indeed and did me no end of good.

"Then one day Wilgar Campbell, my old mate from The Dogs, rang up.'I'm getting this blues jam together, Dave, with Tom Nolan, who played with The Strolling Bones.' I asked him who the bass player was. 'He's a taxi driver who took me to a gig. He lives down my road and it turns out he plays bass. Gary Fletcher'.

"We called the band The Wild Cats. It was fun to play again, but it was very much a jam. It lasted about a year, then one night Tom McGuinness rang me up. I was just on nodding terms with Tom; I'd bumped into him on and off over the years on the blues scene, The 100 Club and places like that. I was still very much in my say 'yes' mode and when he mentioned he was putting this blues thing together, I just said yes. I was back in the laundry van job and one of my deliveries was to Keith Nelson, who'd been in Rock Salt. He'd heard Tom mentioning this proposed Blues project and said 'give Dave Kelly a ring'. I was driving us to a gig one night in the laundry van and I mentioned it to Gary. I suggested he come along to the rehearsal. I'd heard that Hughie Flint was playing drums, and with Tom that meant McGuinness Flint, so I thought it all seemed very interesting. Tom had said on the phone that 'Paul' was coming along. It meant nothing to me at the time. But when we got to the rehearsal, I said to Gary 'Hey; that bloke looks like the fella from Manfred Mann....' Then I realised it was Paul Jones. It became even more interesting. The original choice of bass player was going to be Gerry MacAvoy, who was with Rory Gallagher, but he couldn't do it. What impressed me at that first rehearsal in Deptford was that Tom and Paul had actually worked things out beforehand; we had arrangements. It wasn't going to be the usual blues jams. This formula, the arrangements, the 'show' element became part of our success. It's also probably the reason why the so-called 'authentic' blues fans don't like us. The rest, you know about. The Dave Kelly Band was a good experience. It was a slog, financially, but that was a good band. I was nowhere near as pushy then as I should have been, but playing was always a question of 'as long as it's getting me off....' then I was happy enjoying everybody else's input. During those years when The

The Dave Kelly Band Mk I: John 'Irish' Earle, Rob, Tom, Dave, Lou and Gary

Dave cuts the mustard with Buddy Guy (pic: BBC)

Blues Band weren't working much we had a great line up in the DK Band. Mick Rogers, Irish Earle, Lou Stonebridge, Ed Deane – a great guitarist – Pete Filleul, Rob, Gary. It was nice fronting my own band.

"Is there a Blues band philosophy? I could jokingly reply and say 'Don't go on after midnight'. The Blues Band are probably different to other Blues bands because we have writers in the line-up, and we work hard at what we do. As the nuts & bolts member, wearing my booking agent/managerial hat, I go to a lot of trouble then get annoyed at what I perceive to be a lack of a professional attitude within the band. And yet, we get to a gig, on time, we're tight, know what we're doing, we do a good show and the crowd love it, and I come away thinking 'well.... there is no *lack of professional attitude* at all....' If you're going to quote me on that, then quote the whole thing. What keeps us together? That's another gag, really. We usually say 'We're joined at the wallet....' Seriously, I've always thought that music is a great way of not having to work for a living, and I still think it. Sure, I'd like to practice more, look at my technique, but I hardly ever pick the guitar up these days unless it's a gig. I suppose I've developed what style I have simply by playing night after night. We have lots of fun on stage. One of our fans, Susan McEwan from Edinburgh, told me that what she found fascinating was the interaction between us all on stage. She's right. We do enjoy what we do. We've mellowed. There's no tension these days. We've got a good crew, Lari, Des, Nicky. As for the future, it could go on and on. I hope so. You know, you spend your life touring, gigging in all sorts of places; in England it's been pubs, clubs, then festivals, theatres. But touring Europe with Dire Straits, walking out onto that stage with forty thousand people; I know what you'd say – 'Ah, but Dave, is that *really* Rock & Roll?' And I say 'Yes!' The comfort, the five star treatment; and playing to all those people every night. That was Rock & Roll, the absolute zenith of my performing career. Give me some more!"

Solo Kelly 1968

One of the Family

The Rob Townsend Story

If those of you who are old enough care to delve back into that almost mythical, seemingly carefree decade, 1960-70, you may well recall the sheer mystery and excitement some bands provoked. We'd had all the big time American Rock we could handle, and after the learning curve of the blues boom it was time for the Brits to take music somewhere else. Today, much of what seemed spiritually world-shattering, all those manifestoes of 'new ways to live' appear as just what they were; the dope-dazed, well-intentioned ramblings of bright young brains, wrapped in cheesecloth and dipped in an insubstantial brew of Eastern philosophy and mild anarchy. The Moody Blues, Edgar Broughton, Jefferson Airplane, they all made us think, albeit in a shallow fashion. Family, however, made you slightly apprehensive; their lyrics were hard to pin down; their style totally off-the-wall, their lead singer, Roger Chapman, violently versatile. And they not only had the usual guitar and drums line-up; they had the strange wizardry of Jim King's oriental saxophone, Ric Grech's violin. Family had the best riffs; I defy anyone to play 'Burlesque' today and remain seated. They had style, power and mystery, and yet, as their erstwhile drummer explains, "it was all far simpler than people thought". This interview with Rob Townsend began at 6pm in his local, The Turk's Head. It finished at 4am the following morning over his dining room table, and had there been time, this sturdy raconteur could have given us a book of his own.

"I was born on the same day as Ringo Starr. Not the same year, I hasten to add. 7.7.47, in Leicester, seven years later than Ringo Starr. All the sevens. Sounds like a blues song. I was an only child. My mother had me when she was 42. My father came from a very large family and he was the eldest son. His mother was married to a Samuel Townsend. After having ten kids, she upped and left him and went up the road to Nottingham. Eventually she met and married another guy, called.... Samuel Townsend. She had one child from that second marriage. I never met her. Eventually Samuel Townsend the second died. My father had an elder brother, but he'd been killed, probably in the First World War. So my father, being the oldest, helped to bring up the rest of the family. This probably explains why I came along quite later. He was a trimmer in the hosiery trade. My mother did various things, but was mainly a charlady. She scrubbed the floors in the local Public Library and the Pub; we were pretty 'down market'; we lived in a house with one outside toilet and one outside tap to be shared by three houses. 19 Crane Street, Leicester. That's where I was born. It's been demolished since.

Eventually, when I left school, I got into the print business. When my father died, through the people I knew my mother managed to get a job in the bookbinding trade. Way before I was born I think she was involved in the boot and shoe industry.

"As a kid at school I wasn't particularly academic. I liked reading and loved history. But maths, sciences; I had to really work at it. I was just an average kid until I reached 11 and went to Secondary School and then I started to do O.K. This wasn't due to any natural ability, it was simply that I started really getting down to the work. I got to the top of the class. But it was very competitive in those days. Once you'd got to the top of the class, you had to try and stay there. History and Art, they were my specialist subjects. My father used to draw me the odd cartoon and picture, and I'd begun to draw and copy photographs.

"Music started when I was ten. My father used to play the piano accordian, very badly. The only time he seemed to play it was on Sunday afternoons. My father wasn't really a drinker, but every Sunday lunchtime, in the best northern tradition, he would put on his muffler and his best suit and go off to the pub for his two pints. He would go there with my uncle, who lived next door. He used to come back and take out the accordian, which he'd obviously been fond of for many years and which annoyed my mother, and play. It wasn't until after many years that I realised that you didn't have to chip the peas from the gravy in a Sunday lunch. My mother would stick to her routine and the Sunday lunch would remain in the oven until dad had finished his playing. By the time the food got to the table the gravy had set firmly around the peas. It wasn't until I left home and got married that I realised that gravy was actually supposed to move.

"Anyway, Dad bought a piano. He wanted me to have lessons but the prospect of this petrified me. I refused to do it. One day he turned up with a drum kit which a guy he worked with had made. It was two little drums and two little cymbals.

"I discovered jazz. I was 11 and listening to Acker Bilk and Kenny Ball. I got a plastic clarinet for Christmas and my cousin was a jazz fanatic; Bunk Johnson, Sydney Bechet, Kid Ory. Real traditional stuff. When I was 12 we moved house.

"Every Sunday I would make this pilgrimage, which was two good bus rides, to my cousin's house. He'd be out, but he had a record player. All his records were there and I'd play them; Bunk, Bechet, Ory. Lovely, exciting music. At the same time the woman next door gave me a cross between a mandolin and a banjo; a banjolele. I loved it. It was real George Formby. I was hooked. One of my other cousins had a five string, full-scale banjo, and I borrowed that. I started learning chords, learning 'Swanee River' and all that. My cousin with the jazz records, Johnny Varnam, became my total mentor. Him and his girlfriend began taking me to see jazz artistes. I saw Chris Barber, Acker Bilk, lots of others. And I was still wearing my school cap and short trousers. Here was Johnny, courting this woman, saying 'I'm bringing my nephew along' and I'd arrive dressed like that. How they ever got married with me constantly turning up I'll never know....

"Of course, at that time, Acker Bilk wasn't *Stranger on The Shore* and all that crap; he was playing good, hard New Orleans music. He had a banjo player called Roy James and he did this number – I think it was called *Rent House Stomp*. There I was, sitting in my short trousers in the De Montfort Hall in Leicester, watching this man play this incredible

banjo solo, and it dawned on me; I would never ever be able to play like that. I looked at my stumpy little fingers and thought; 'No way....'

"The drummer was a guy called Ron McKay and I suddenly thought about that drum kit at home; 'I can do that', I said to myself. The banjo went out of the window. Unfortunately I knew very little about drumming. Ron McKay turned out to be left-footed and right-handed, so for ages I played this extremely weird drum kit which was totally back to front because I'm right-handed and right-footed. McKay became my idol. I still didn't have a record player, so I had to wait patiently for my parents to go out, then rush into the living room and put the radio on and play along with it. It was the same when we got TV; if a drummer appeared and mum and dad were out I'd bring my kit in and play along. I was totally hooked.

"When I was 13, I remember that Christmas I got a snare drum and a pair of drum sticks. Up to then all I'd had were these wire brushes which came with the home-made kit. Every year, for our holidays, we'd go to the same place; Mrs. Daley's, Victoria Road, Mablethorpe. One night on holiday, although, as I've said, my father wasn't really a drinker, we went into the Mablethorpe Labour Club. They had a piano and drummer. The drummer had a snare drum, a bass drum and a hi-hat. Well, I'd never played a bass drum or a hi-hat before. My dad came over and I reckon he'd had one pint too many (three by now), he said 'Come on. I've told 'em you're playing the drums and they've bet me you can't so you're off on the stage'. I told him I couldn't. He replied that I mustn't let him down.... so I gave in and, terrified, got up there. I played with the pianist, the drummer was relieved. As soon as I got behind that kit – that was it. I was on every night that week.

"I was excited when I got back to Leicester. I recall that I'd broken the skin on my snare drum and I'd no idea how to repair it. I took it to our local music shop, Moore and Stanworth. The older partner, Mr. Stanworth, had been a jazzer at some time. He took the drum from me and said 'Yes, I can change the skin; come back in a week'. I went back with my mother on the Friday and he said 'I've repaired your drum, but if you're really taking this seriously, it's not the drum you should be playing....' Well, we didn't have any money. I asked him what drum I ought to play. He showed me a second hand

Rob drumming furiously in the early '60s Leicester band, The Torrents

Top of the Town: Leicester Town Hall steps playing host to the Beatniks

Premier snare. It looked awful to me; my drum was all stardust and glittery, this had been a pearly white but had absorbed tobacco stains to turn it a sickly beige. I learned later, of course, that not only were Premier great drums, but that they were actually made in Leicester at the time!

"Until I left school that guy, Mr. Stanworth, was great. I recall going in there when I desperately needed a bass pedal discovering it was twenty five pounds, which was a fortune. He let me pay for it in instalments.... even though I was under aged; no written agreements – he simply trusted me.

"Another crucial point after Mablethorpe was seeing a Gene Krupa movie on TV. I just knew this was what I'd wanted to do. I was still a bit aloof with my musical tastes. I was reading the *Melody Maker* when all the kids at school were reading the Musical Express. I thought pop was rubbish; until, one day, coming home from school on the top deck of the bus one of my mates was carrying a transistor radio – even that was quite flash in those days. I heard this terrific music, and asked him what it was. He was surprised. 'What is it!? It's only number one in the charts! This is the Shadows – *Apache!*'

"I was impressed with the drumming. Tony Meehan became an instant hero. Although he was with The Shadows, a pop group, I discovered that he was influenced by Joe Morello, Dave Brubeck's drummer. So, as far as I was concerned, Meehan was on a par with me because of his interest in jazz.

"I thought I needed lessons, and I discovered to my surprise that the caretaker at my school was a drummer with the local Palais dance band – and he read music. I told him I wanted to learn to play properly and he began giving me lessons down in the school boiler room at lunchtimes. I'd just take along my sticks and a practice pad and off went, learning rolls and paradiddles. Eventually, I went to his house with my new snare drum and hi-hat. He told me I needed a bass drum, but I disagreed. I said I needed a tom-tom. He said 'Why'? I said 'So I can play *Apache!*'

"The outcome was that my hard-pressed mother and I turned up yet again at Stanworth's shop and she bought me a bass drum – a huge thing – for twelve pounds. I found out later that she used to hive away what she could from the housekeeping money for my drumming requirements, and my father, who considered himself to be the musician in the house, when he found out about it, went berserk. Even so, until the day my mother passed away, which was only 1987, she would still ask me 'When are you going to get yourself a real job'? But she had always encouraged me.

"I eventually got to see Count Basie, Duke Ellington, and, ultimately, The Shadows, but Tony Meehan had been replaced on drums by Brian Bennet. Bennet didn't seem to play anything like the records. I was still split; I knew to make money you needed to play in a group in a pub. I joined a school band, doing the youth clubs, the odd pub. I used to get rope-burns on my hands through carrying my drums in cardboard boxes tied up with string on the bus! Then I met a guy called Buzz Ford, who fronted a band called The Classics. They were all older than me, in their twenties, and they had an audition to play at Butlin's holiday camps. I was invited to do the audition and I got the job. We were due to go to and play at Butlin's in Skegness. My mum wouldn't let me leave school and go. They couldn't get another drummer so they didn't go anyway, but I still joined them.

"We started doing the clubs and pubs and I became known as *The Grapefruit Kid*. Depending on where we were playing, pub or club, because I was under age, I had to stay out of the way when we weren't actually playing, and drink my grapefruit juice, either at a discrete table or in the little room at the side of the stage. Buzz Ford played guitar and piano, and although we played the current hit parade, we also played (because they seemed so 'old' to me) lots of Little Richard and Jerry Lee Lewis. So it was Buzz who taught me how to play with a piano.

"Eventually the band broke up for various reasons; a girl singer joined, and we seemed to change direction. The bass player, John Davis, went to join an established working men's club band called Gus Horsepool and the Beatniks. The drummer's job in that band came up; he put the word in for me and I got the job. Gus Horsepool was a piano player too, so again it was Jerry Lee Lewis and Little Richard. I remember asking Gus once, 'Gus Horsepool – is that your real name?' He said 'No, that's just my stage name.' So I said 'Ah.... I see. So what's your real name?' He said 'My real name is Melvyn Horsepool'! While I was with the Beatniks I was made a very impressive offer to go pro. We supported

Leicester's finest: The Broodly Hoo. Left to right: Rob, Stu Milton, Phil Wright (now with Steve Gibbons), 'Zoot', and 'Jim'

Johnny Kidd & The Pirates on one of his tour dates. When we came off stage, Kidd pulled me aside and offered me the job drumming with The Pirates. I went home, all excited, but my mum hit the roof. As far as she was concerned, I was finishing my schooling and finishing it properly. 'You're not going down to London and doing all that silly stuff!' she said, in no uncertain terms. Still, I was offered a job with Johnny Kidd, and that seemed pretty impressive. Mind you, it might not have been such a good move. About nine months later Johnny Kidd was dead. But I did get to play with the great Mick Green, the Pirate's guitarist, years later. But I digress....

"So, it was back to the Beatniks. Old Gus is still working; does a lot of work for kids now. We used to try and play blues and stuff. We'd been to the El Rondo ballroom in Silver Street, Leicester one Saturday. I saw a band called The Rolling Stones. I'd just left school and got my 'O' levels. It was a small, claustrophobic venue; sweat running down the walls, and I saw the Stones and was amazed. I

thought 'That's it. I wanna do that.'

"Their single *Come On* had just been released, and they did an encore – twice – *Bye Bye Johnny*; I was sold. The young bands scene was beginning in Leicester. My band were in their twenties and I was still fifteen. An ad appeared in the paper for a band called the Farinas; the word was that they were going to make it. I think it was either Philips records or Decca who held some auditions for new bands at the Corn Exchange in Leicester. The search was on for the new Beatles. I went along with The Beatniks, six o'clock one night. I was trying to influence this older band. We wanted to wear black leather waistcoats like The Stones but we couldn't afford them, so we turned up in black trousers and herringbone waistcoats that we'd bought on Leicester market. We did our four numbers, then a band from Peterborough, The Gentry, came on. They were bloody good. I knew that the Farinas were going to be on that night. I also knew that the Farina's guitarist, Charlie Whitney, had been at that Stone's gig.

Family, in their original glory: Grech, Townsend, Whitney, Chappo and the exotic Jim King

Anyway, at the Corn Exchange there was one weirdly dressed guy in the crowd in a long overcoat and trilby hat. Everybody else was trying to look like the Beatles but this guy seemed different. The MC called out *'The Farinas!'* and this guy took his hat and coat off; it was Jim King. They played 'Bo Diddley' like I'd never heard it before. I thought 'Bloody hell!' There was Jim King, Charlie Whitney, a drummer called Harry Overenall; can't remember the bass player. It had a great affect on me.

"There was a coffee shop in town where you usually went with your mum on Saturdays when you were shopping. They started to open this place up on odd nights as a rock venue. A band appeared there called The Broodly Hoo. The buzz was, if you couldn't get to see the Farinas, you saw the 'Broods'. I got a phone call from Charlie Whitney. He'd started a booking agency called Klock Agency. They were booking the Broodlies and the drummer was ill. Whitney had seen me somewhere on the scene and he asked me to dep for him. I went to the coffee bar gig and we were playing blues and stuff. It was great, but I only had three gigs and the drummer

returned.

"One day a guy came to my house. A singer called Phil Wright – he's with Steve Gibbons now – he said 'I'm with the Broodlies; we're sacking Mort, the drummer, and we'd like you to join.' Suddenly I was in a different area of music; there was some soul, Tamla stuff, alongside the blues material. They were into the whole 'mod' thing; back-combed hair; I became a semi-mod overnight. Dress sense dawned on me. I had to keep up with them – they were 'the kiddies'. We used to all congregate around the same record shop; looking for imports, rehearsing the material and surprising the audience with our sharp renditions of these great new tracks. Phil Wright let me borrow a record player. I was sixteen, in work in a graphics studio. My father had a bad heart and suddenly he passed away.

"During the last year at school, doing well at art, a new teacher, Derek Green, came along, and he changed my life. It was Derek who saw my artistic potential, and he got me to go to nightclasses, which he ran. I was bowled over by him. He was from London and he wore a leather tie – he was young and during the lessons at nightclass he would bring in a record player. I'd bought my very first record; Tommy Tucker's *High Heel Sneakers* which blew me away. Derek Green wanted me to go to Art College but with my father dying I wanted to work, but really I wanted to play music. Derek Green got me the job in the graphics studio.

"The Broodly Hoo expanded; we got organ, brass; we played *In the Midnight Hour* and people were impressed. Charlie Whitney called me again. He was still one of the big boys on the Leicester scene. Whitney was interested in what I was doing, and I'd got to know the Farina's drummer – a great player, Harry Overenall. We were doing a Brood's gig down the road from Leicester University, and when we'd finished we went along there to see the Farinas. I remember walking into the hall and there was Jim King playing fabulous harmonica – he reminded me of Sonny Boy Williamson – and Ric Grech was singing *All-Night Worker*, and I thought 'Oh.... hell – no! I'm still going in the wrong direction!'

"To cut an even longer story short, the Broodly Hoo broke up as the lads all started going off to University. Just before they split, another band came on the scene, named after their drummer, Le Gay. Sounds funny now, I know, but that was the name. They could hardly play at all, but they were doing all this Tamla stuff. They were just a 4-piece, but what they had going for them was that they were all pretty; very good looking lads. The drummer suffered with ulcers. Le Gay used to throw up in the middle of a performance. The keyboard player had taught himself. He worked in the same graphics studio as me. With Le Gay being ill, they asked me to stand in one night at a cellar club gig in Leicester.

"With the Broods I'd been a bit restricted because of the line-up of the band, what with the organ, brass and stuff. But when I played with Le Gay, I was unfettered; I had the time of my life. It was like The Who, and they'd just become very popular then. They all had outrageous hairdos and the girls all turned up and I thought 'Oh.... yeah! This is it!' Anyway, their poor old drummer was too ill and they had to let him go. They asked me to join. They thought that because I had a bit more 'cred' after being with the Broods, and I could play a bit better – although not a lot – I'd give the band a slightly better profile. The local paper had this headline, something like 'Townsend finds freedom'; I was at

work and picked up the paper and thought '*Whaaat*!?'

"At the time the Broods broke up, we'd been playing a residency at, no less, the Flamingo in London. We used to travel down once a week. Although I was getting promoted at work, I'd lost interest in the job, because I'd long since decided that music was my career. And no-one from Leicester became 'musicians'! It was unheard of. I was playing all over the country, arriving back in the morning from places like Sunderland and being too late for work. The residency at the Flamingo had blown it for me at the day job. It meant me leaving work at four on a Friday, the Broodlies still being at school had already left. I used to tell the boss I was going for regular dental treatment until I was called in one day; the local paper had this piece about us playing the big time in London. He wasn't best pleased. I knew I was on the way out; it was just a matter of time.

"I'd been sent to night-class by the firm to study typography, and halfway through the class I used to bunk off down to the El Rondo and watch jazz. One night I saw John Mayall's Bluesbreakers; Clapton was with them; end of story. It was the biggest case of 'This is it!' in my career to date. I wasn't too happy about the appearance of the drummer, this ugly little bloke with a goatee beard. I'd seen the *Beano* album and I thought 'That bloke's got a beard! He looks like a jazzer and he ought to look like Eric!' So there was Eric, bending notes. I'd seen Eric before with the Yardbirds, but this Mayall appearance was something else. Eventually, the ugly little drummer with the goatee turned from a frog into a prince; he's now very handsome and a very nice bloke and I love him dearly, like a father.... Hughie.

"I saw the Downliner's Sect, Steampacket, Alex Harvey, Rod Stewart, Julie Driscoll. It was so exciting. I still didn't have my own record player, but I still had the borrowed one, and someone lent me a Mose Allison album. I was even more enthusiastically confused. Eventually I had to return the borrowed record player but once again my mum came to the rescue; she bought me a blue Dansette, and I had that machine still when I was well into my days with Family. In fact it was Carol, my wife, who bought a stereo and made me chuck out the Dansette. I recall that when we were in Family, if we got fresh pressings of a single or an LP, Whitney and Chappo got a copy, because they had sophisticated equipment, but I got a copy just so we could hear what Family sounded like to the ordinary punter with the little record player!

"Not long after Le Gay, Cream started to happen and the Flower Power thing began to drift in. People with fresh ideas; some with completely no ideas. The Farinas, in Leicester, had now changed their name to The Roaring Sixties. They began to make a name for themselves in London. I would bump into Whitney at gigs.

"One day, I had the flu. I was off work with a genuine reason, for a change. There was a knock at the door; it was Ric Grech from The Roaring Sixties. He'd come to ask me to join the band. I asked him what was to happen to their regular drummer, Harry; Rick just told me he 'was to leave....'. Roger Chapman seemed a dark, fascinating character. For a start, he was twenty five; it seemed that those three years meant so much; me approaching 23. Chappo had a reputation in Leicester. He'd already been pro, worked in Germany. He wasn't known as an easy touch; he seemed hard, with tattoos and a worldly way, to say nothing of that unique voice. He wasn't a man you messed with, but I've found since that he didn't deserve a lot of that; he wasn't a soft touch, no, but he is a very nice man.

"The day-job was the last thing on my mind. My mother had given up on me. I'd been scouring the papers for a part-time job and she knew the writing was on the wall. The Roaring Sixties came to a Le Gay gig on a Saturday night, an open air event in a marquee. Afterwards they told me to make my mind up. The next morning I rang them from a phone box, and I was in. Rehearsals were called for 11 the next morning, which was a Monday. Of course, I was late in to work the next morning. I walked past the boss's office and he called out 'Hey! I want a word with you!' The word he'd planned was simply about being late. My words were different. He took me into the reception area. I said that I'd been offered a job. He said 'You'd better take it....' I said 'Er.... there's one problem; I have to go to London – this morning....' Actually, I only had to go just around the corner to rehearse with what by now had become Family. They'd already changed their name and cut their first single. The boss just glared at me and said 'Well.... go, then!'

"The odd thing about that moment was that I thought I'd made it very clear that I was finished and wasn't coming back. The boss said as far as he was concerned I hadn't done it properly; it was as if he still had some hold over me because I was in London six months later and he still wouldn't let go of my P45! Still, that morning was a watershed in many ways.

"I remember leaving the building and looking at my watch, I had time for a coffee, and I was thinking 'Hey! It's a whole hour to go before I start work....'

"Family's drummer, for whom I had the greatest respect and admiration, Harry Overenall, had left because of the direction the band were going in. They'd been listening to John Peel and Pirate Radio, and they wanted to do something original. Harry simply wanted to carry on playing straight R&B, and it felt strange, after he'd been such an influence, to be taking his place. Still, this was it. I felt as if it was finally happening. This wasn't to say that Le Gay didn't carry on; they had that something that we all had; determination. I saw them on *Top of The Pops* quite a while after I'd left. I learnt much later that the singer had died of cancer. It's a pity. They were such good lads.

"When I joined Family, Jim King was still doing Sonny Boy Williamson stuff, as well as all the more esoteric material. In fact, looking back and thinking about the attitude of some of the 'Blues anoraks', I reckon I've as much right to be in The Blues Band as anyone. I was expected to know and play Howlin' Wolf material. Family were a blues band, but it was what they were doing with the music which made the difference. Do you know there's a song on the album, *A Song For Me* that started out as *How Many More Years*. I get credited on that track because we started out with it as a jam and it evolved into something else, but it was the blues that gave it birth. I had to learn J. B. Lenoir songs, and I've toured with Memphis Slim. Yet there are still those people out there who think my background is all psychedelic. Well, it isn't; it's the blues.

"I always remember doing the Memphis Slim tour. There was me, a bass player who I can't remember, and the late Duster Bennett. We rehearsed for about two hours at Ronnie Scott's club. The tour manager asked me back to his place for a drink after the rehearsal. He said 'Memphis is not happy....' I was worried. Was it me? I was known in England at that time, just after Family, as a rock

Family Mk II: Roger Chapman, John Wetton, Charlie Whitney, Polly Palmer, Rob Townsend

drummer. So was it me? 'No.... Memphis says you're not a straight blues drummer but a jazz/blues drummer, and that suits him fine. It's Duster Bennett he's not happy with....' I was taken aback. Duster Bennett, who'd spent all his life learning how to play blues! So you see, it's not as clear cut as the anoraks like to think. It's all to do with serving your apprenticeship, learning your trade. Dave Kelly often has a gentle aside about me playing with Duane Eddy. But I've got a letter from Duane telling me I was better than the original Rebel Rousers. When I was at school, Duane Eddy was up there in the guitar hero stakes with the likes of Hank Marvin, and I ended up playing in his band. And you should hear his banjo playing.... a very nice man.

"Family was an exciting time. I'd joined in the *Summer of Love*. The Beatles were huge. We were still mixing the blues with our own stuff. *The Doll's House* album came out. We had a mix of producers on that album. We started off with Jimmy Miller, who was also working with the Stones. Then Dave Mason was brought in from Traffic. Eddie Kramer, the Beatle's engineer, did his bit. It sold well. Our manager, John Gilbert, was the son of the famous film director, Lewis Gilbert. He had a lot to do with that unusual sleeve, because of his film connections. The album was released on Warner Reprise – in which Frank Sinatra had a large interest. The idea was to release the album in the States, then import it, because everyone was crying out for imported US albums. Rolling Stone magazine slammed it, although when they interviewed me years later they called it *'Family's all-time classic'* and I curtly reminded them what a panning they'd given it at the time! I've always made it a policy to just keep the bad reviews, not the good ones. The guy at Rolling Stone got a shock when I produced their crap review. Mind you, it was the Family album I really

The Irish experience: The Band meets Noel Redding (far right)

hated. I was into all that 'different' material, but like Chappo, I was basically a Muddy Waters, Howlin' Wolf, Rock'n'Roll fan. The critics read all sorts of stuff into the band's lyrics. But it was simple and uncomplicated; we weren't writing any complicated political agendas, just lyrics that hung together and performed well.

"Those early days in London were wonderful. Our Manager had brought us down and installed us in a house, 40 Lots Road, Worlds End, Chelsea. Two doors away there lived another band, Mighty Baby; (they used to be known as The Action). They couldn't afford the electricity in their house, so we got our roadies to run power cables from ours. On the other side of us was Victor Brox, who was playing at the time with Aynsley Dunbar's Retaliation. These people were always dropping around.

"We went on our first foreign tour, around Europe, with The Byrds. We got quite friendly with Gram Parsons. I remember waking up at Lots Road in the early hours and Roger Chapman's room was throbbing with noise. I thought he'd got his stereo full on. I wasn't quite totally untamed 'rock'n'roll' at this stage. I was still wearing my sensible Marks & Spencer's pyjamas. I got up and burst into Chappo's room to berate him and there was Gram Parsons, Doug Dillard on banjo and other legends all sat playing. I retired gracefully, aware of what a rare moment it had been. They were good days.

"Then came the first American tour, which was a disaster, due to a misunderstanding concerning the promoter, Bill Graham, who ran the Fillmore East and West, Roger Chapman and a mike stand. Graham had fallen out of favour with the hippie movement. When Chapman threw the mike stand, it narrowly missed Graham's head, and he thought Family were out to make a quick name for themselves by killing him! A lot was written about that incident, so, for the record, here's what happened; I know, because I was there.

"To begin with, there was some tension anyway. I think the tour was called *The English Invasion*. Ten Years After were headlining, and there was The Nice and Hendrix. Bill Graham had already asked The Nice not to burn the American flag when they performed Leonard Bernstein's *America*. You recall they used to reach the middle of the tune then Emerson would set fire to the Stars & Stripes on stage. Well, Lee Jackson, the Nice's bassist, had assured Graham that the flag burning wouldn't happen. The rest of the gigs on the tour were conditional on how we went down there, at the Fillmore East. The audience was full of acid freaks who kept running about. To make things worse, just before we were due to go on, Ric Grech informed us he was leaving to join Blind Faith. He couldn't tell us in Britain, no. He saved it until we arrived in New York. Well, The Nice went on, and you guessed it, they ignored Graham's request and burned the flag anyway. Graham was not amused. Then we went on, Chapman went into one of his passionate bouts of excitement, lost control, threw the mike stand, and that was us – off. Graham said we were banned off the tour, but a deputation went to him; the Hendrix band, Ten Years After, they all remonstrated with him and the compromise was that our name would be taken from the posters, our photograph removed from the foyers; in fact we were obliterated; nobody knew we were on the tour until we took the stage. Years later we played for Bill Graham in San Francisco and it was all forgotten.

"We did other tours over there; with Savoy Brown when they were big, and another superb tour with Elton John. Elton was a smashing bloke. I remember his American manager telling us to come off and not do any encores. The first night we obeyed the rule, we'd gone down really well and we went off. The crowd were stomping, Elton came into the dressing room and said 'What're you doing?' We told him we'd been told 'no encores'. Elton told us to go out there and do one, so we did. When we came backstage again, he had a bottle of champagne waiting for us. 'You boys played a blinder tonight and you deserve this', he said. 'I don't ever want to hear you say you can't do an encore – tell the manager to sod off. I brought you on this tour because you play so well, when my boys go on stage they have to play out of their skins because you've blown them off!'

"That was a nice tour, three months. Yet during that tour something was going wrong; we weren't enjoying playing as much as we should and it was all down to just one member of the band. I don't want any lawsuits, but he was replaced. We phoned back to England and got a new member; Tony Ashton, (later of Ashton, Gardner & Dyke). But by this time, although we were still on a high, we knew it was in some way winding down. We'd been at it five years, and Whitney & Chapman were writing material they thought wasn't suitable for Family, but they still wanted it on the market. During that last year, with Tony Ashton, Family was turned around; it became a fun band to be in.

"We came back to England and did a festival with Beck, Bogart and Appice – remember them? They followed us on stage and they blew the place apart. I'd always admired Carmen Appice anyway, but boy,

did they play a blinder. Back at the hotel, I said to the rest of the guys, 'Do you realise – that was the same kind of fire we used to play with five years ago....' and we all just knew it was over. There was no animosity; we simply agreed we would wind it up. The next night we were topping the bill, and we played up a storm. It was as if all the pressure had gone; we knew we were packing it in and we played with all the passion we'd had in the early days. It was a great final year. We didn't even care about what the press said anymore, and there was always a section of the music press who gave us a hard time. It was the crowd you didn't buy drinks for at The Speakeasy – people you didn't know. They'd go away and put the boot in. We'd often read crap reviews written by people who we very well knew were not at the gig. Unfortunately, if it's in the papers, people believe it.

"We had some people on our side; Nick Logan, for instance. We did one concert not long after Chappo had had an ear & throat operation. Nick Logan wrote a good piece, saying he'd seen us play better, yet he still found space to be positive. Fair and accurate criticism – it beats lies every time. When we played the Roundhouse in London once, the *Melody Maker* referred to us as 'the poor man's Slade'! The guy who wrote the review had actually been carried out of the gig blind drunk before we'd actually arrived on stage! Two weeks later, at Knebworth, one of his fellow *MM* scribes came up to us and apologised. Great; too late to tell the public; we were the poor man's Slade, whether he'd seen us or not.

"We were all getting involved in other things by this time. Tony Ashton had produced a couple of hit records for Medicine Head. At that time they were just a duo; now they decided to become a band of sorts. Carol and I had just had a son arrive on the scene. Chappo and Whitney wanted to lay off for six months to produce songs for an album. Well, they could afford to, but not being a writer, I couldn't afford to stop playing. So, I joined Medicine Head. As it happened, the very first track I played on with them, *Slip & Slide*, was a hit, so by the time Whitney & Chapman had their Streetwalkers album out, I was well established with Medicine Head. Unfortunately, we didn't have another hit.

"I was asked to tour with a man who to me was, and always will be, a rock legend, Duane Eddy. This was the mid-seventies and Duane had been out of practice, but that tour was great. A nice man. I was by now looking for session work. I played on all sorts of records. I even did the Eurovision Song; can't remember the poor girl's name, but when we recorded it I did it as a reggae beat. On competition night she had to sing with the Euro house orchestra and their drummer just played it as straight rock. Disaster.

"I also worked with a good songwriter, Philip Goodhand-Tait. I was busy recording an album with him, whilst at the same time rehearsing for a live TV show with a Newcastle Band called Splinter, I was also doing jingles. I'd be in a studio until eleven at night, then off to the station, train to Newcastle, in the TV studios at nine the next morning.... drums in a taxi.... then back to London for the next session. I was existing on the odd couple of hour's sleep. I woke up one day in agony with blood pouring from my ear. The trouble is, with session work, you work your way to the top of the list and then, if you turn a job down for whatever reason, the guy behind you, who's usually a damn good player, as most session people are, gets the job. You go back to the end of the queue. I knew I'd been pushing it, and I also knew that session work wasn't for me, because I have to totally believe one hundred percent in what I'm playing; you can't always feel that commitment in a jingle for High-Speed Gas.

"I began to realise I was getting older when I watched *Top of The Pops* one night. I recognised the drumming on a record – it was my drumming yet here was this band on the screen with an eighteen year old kid miming to my work! I thought, you bastards – *Top of The Pops*, I'm on the record, yet you don't call me up. But that was what you were in session work; anonymous.

"Muff Winwood hired me for one session with Kevin Ayers, and I'd been called in to do the album. I worked with a bass player called Charlie McCracken who used to be with Taste – Rory Gallagher's band. Charlie and I became good friends. The Ayers album, *Yes, We have no Mañanas* turned out really nice. Kevin Ayers was a dream to work with, a super bloke.

"At this point Ric Grech had come back from the States where he'd been writing with Gram Parsons. He rang me and asked if I'd like to come and record with him, bringing a bass player (Charlie), with the

idea of forming a band. Now he'd got a reputation for being into certain substances but I'd been assured he was 'clean'. I went up to Leicester to sound things out. He wanted to form a country band and we sat down one Saturday afternoon and he played me some tapes. I hated country music at this time, but the stuff he was playing me was great. So, we went into the studio. The first song we put down was *Jolene*, long before it became a hit.

"But although Ric was off the drugs, he was on the booze. He began to take over the sessions, and in spite of the fact that this was the man who'd originally come around to our house to ask me to join Family, I couldn't put up with all that again. He just wanted to dominate and get to wherever he wanted to be at any expense, but I thought.... 'No'. Even though there was mega money and a big, big manager behind Grech, Charlie and I decided to go with Kevin Ayers; reason: he was a nice man.

"The Ayers band was a nice project; we had Zoot Money on Keyboards and Andy Summers, who later joined the Police, on guitar. Kevin Ayers was from a totally different background to us. He loved life and was a joy to be with. His Grandfather is responsible for the dimensions of the modern cricket bat, and his father was a pioneer in the field of live TV entertainment, bringing a magazine type Saturday show to BBC2 in the early days. Kevin was classically trained and the whole period was musically taxing, being as I am an untrained player. You wouldn't have got a good player like Andy Summers interested either, if there hadn't been something particularly interesting to get your teeth into. Yes, the whole Kevin Ayers thing was a very happy time.

"Shortly after this I got to know Derek Taylor, who'd been given a big office at Warner Brothers, possibly due to his connection with The Beatles, in the hope that he might lure one of the fab four to the label. Derek was a charming man. His first signing to the label surprised everybody; it was George Melly. He called another meeting a few weeks later.... a rock band? No; he'd signed Spike Milligan! The reason it was open house there, especially for me, was that Carol, my wife, worked there. Derek introduced me to Peter Skellern, who'd just had a number one with *You're a Lady*. He got me a session the following day – I remember it because I was playing congas and the guitar player was the great Albert Lee, who I'd first seen years back when I was with the Beatniks and he topped a bill I was on, playing for Chris Farlowe; I even remember the song; they did Hooker's *Boom Boom*.

"The next session Skellern offered me was more tricky; I turned it down because he was a classically trained pianist and I simply didn't read music. But he talked me into it. He said it was simple; just a trio. When I got to the studio, I noticed eighty chairs set up. No sign of Skellern. I checked with one of the guys, who said he was in the bar. Eventually Skellern appeared with this other guy, who he introduced to me; 'This is the conductor for the night....' I was taken aback. 'Conductor? What is all this?' Peter said he'd decided to have the whole London Philharmonic Orchestra on the track, and here they were! In spite of the fact I couldn't read music, Peter Skellern got me through it by explaining carefully what he wanted and nodding at the right times. I was petrified; it was a large whisky in the bar that night, but at least I'd played with the LSO. I did quite a bit of work with Peter, along with the bass player George Forde, who was Emile Forde's brother and one of the original Checkmates. We were on the single *Hold On To Love* and we did an album, too, plus some big shows.

"The Kevin Ayers thing fell apart because Kevin took a long holiday and forgot to come back. John Reed, Elton John's manager, had found this Irish guy who he thought was pretty good. They put me, Andy Summers and Billy Livesey in the studio with him, and I thought it might go somewhere. I said to Andy 'What do you reckon?' He had other ideas. 'Well, Rob.... I've been messing around with this band down at the Marquee.... it's a punk band....'

"I found that hysterical. 'Give over, Summers!' I said, 'A man of your age?!' Now remember, he's older than me. I'd been to see him with Zoot Money's Big Roll Band when I was a teenager and just left school. But that punk band was The Police, and I used to pick up the Daily Mirror and read stuff like *Andy Summers, 30, guitarist with supergroup, the Police....* Funny, I thought.... I'm 35.... good luck to him.

"The 1980s approached. It was a lean period. Drum machines had crept in and drumming, live drumming, which I prefer, had to conform to so many beats per minute to meet the 'dance formula'. One day I was waiting in Waterloo Station and I bumped into Lou Stonebridge and Tom McGuinness. I'd met Tom before, having done gigs with Medicine Head alongside McGuinness Flint. They invited me to play at a gig they were doing in

Slip and Slide: Rob joins Medicine Head

my local pub, The Turk's Head. This turned into a monthly thing. Hughie Flint turned up occasionally and we'd have two drummers. Paul turned up and I got to play a Bob Dylan song, (Dylan being my hero) *If you've got to go*; it was free and easy, we got tighter, even had a brass section some nights. Then Tom and Paul left; they'd formed The Blues Band. So Lou Stonebridge, myself and the rest of us, with brass, ended up playing soul; Stax, that kind of stuff. The Blues Band asked us if we fancied touring with them, so we reckoned if they were called The Blues Band, then we'd be The Dance Band. And so we went out on that first tour, The Spring Cruise Tour.

"After that period I lost touch briefly with The Blues Band, but I remember driving home with McCracken one night through Putney. As we passed the Half Moon, I saw this huge queue around the block. I asked if he knew who was playing that night, he said 'Yeah.... it's a band called The Blues Band....' I was amazed.

"Then one night in 1981 I got a call from Tom McGuinness, who told me that Hughie was quitting The Blues Band and would I be up for the gig? I had this record deal with the Dance Band and although it was difficult at the time with people leaving, etc, I felt I owed it to them to stay. Another thing was that I really didn't think that The Blues Band were very.... well, 'big'. But that Christmas things got worse with The Dance Band. I went to Lou's New Year's day party and Gary Fletcher was there. He started telling me that he'd been touring continuously for two years, Scandinavia, Canada, Germany.... I thought; hang on – this is a big band.... So I asked him if the job was still open. 'Sorry Rob.... but we're holding auditions. They start tomorrow and we've got forty guys lined up. You could try phoning the office....' I did. I spoke to Gilly Tarrant and I got my audition, although I failed the first one. I got asked back and made it the second time. The rest you know about.

"So there you have it. Have I a philosophy? I suppose it's just to keep playing, as long as I can just earn enough to support my family. It's not been a money-based career anyway. I play because I enjoy it; playing live music is what I always wanted to do, and if I end up drumming away for twenty five quid a night, then so be it. I remember auditioning for McCartney and not getting the job, yet I went out and celebrated. You see, if I ever got to that level, I'd

want to do it with guys who'd gone through it all like I have. People always expect you to go for promotion in any job. But I don't want anything that spectacular. Are you making enough to live on, and are you happy doing what you do? Those are the questions. I remember playing with Medicine Head in the early '70s and earning a hundred quid a week. That was a good wage then. But I got a phone call from Family's manager, and he said 'I've got you a job as Marc Bolan's drummer'. Bolan was hot stuff then. I said, 'But I'm with Medicine Head....' He said, 'forget that shit – this is good money. Bolan's big.' Now Family's manager was my son's Godfather, but he said 'if you don't take this job I'll never speak to you again'. And he didn't. Not for many years, anyway.

"We went on tour in Germany with Medicine Head and on the very first date I got a phone call in my hotel. It was Bolan's manager. 'Big world tour, Rob. We want you to do it. Two hundred and fifty quid a week'. But I didn't go. Sure, there's a price to pay for all that, but as I say, money isn't the reason I play. And even though McCartney turned me down, I got a phone call from his brother, Mike. Paul had recommended me to gig and record with The Scaffold, so I did. Something came of it after all. But I like to like the people and the music I'm involved with. I've seen so many bands where the bass player hates the guitarist and the drummer hates the singer, but they go on stage and put on this big front because they're earning megabucks. But it's not like that for me. I like the guys in The Blues Band. I like the music.

"The future? Bop till we drop? Why not. I remember Paul being on 'Parkinson' with Roger Daltrey. We'd just played a storming headliner at a Brussels festival, and here was Michael Parkinson saying to Daltrey and Paul Jones 'Don't you think you're a little old now for all this?' Paul said 'Funny. How come you don't ask B. B. King that?' And that is exactly how I feel about the business. There is no 'end'. Do you know, I don't even have a pension fund. I've never even thought about it. I never thought about a pension thirty years ago in Leicester, and frankly, I've not had time to think about one since. Hopefully I'll be too busy playing to get around to it...."

"Everything: from Hamlet to Joseph"

The Paul Jones Story

Because of Paul Jones, The Blues Band were never a 'lad's' band. The unique combination of his glamour, excellent musical and vocal ability and media profile in tandem with the chainsaw, take-no-prisoners thrust of his co-front man, Dave Kelly, assured the correct mix of audience crucial to the growth and continuance of a popular band. But the theatre-goers, lovers of musicals and autograph-hunters should make no mistake; the bedrock of this man's career is, and has always been, his love of the Blues.

The Blues cost him his education at Oxford, but elevated him to almost icon status by the late 1960s. To call Paul Jones a 'professional' is a gross understatement. Whatever he does he does with panache, dedication and precision; acting, singing, writing, broadcasting; and playing the harmonica.

Paul Jones, or as he was, Paul Pond, was born in Portsmouth in 1942. His late father was a Captain in the Royal Navy.

"My father was very much a self-made man. He had working class origins, joined the Royal Navy as an Ordinary Seaman and worked his way up to become a Captain, which was quite an achievement. I remember fondly as a boy how he used to read 'Self-made man' stories to me out of the Sunday papers. He would say; 'Did you know that Charles Clore was once a shoe shine boy?' I would say 'Well, I never did, er, who's Charles Clore....?" and he would explode with 'Who's Charles Clore!? He's one of the richest men in the world!' And so, whenever I did anything which could be construed as failure, I became pretty unpopular at home, but when I did anything which approached success, I was very much 'The Boy'. Since that time in my life I've swung between the two extremes. My older brother became a Church of England Minister – a Vicar – and is now the incumbent at a parish in Buckinghamshire.

"He'd also joined the Navy, but somewhat against my father's wishes. Father insisted that the Navy was no career for 'a sensitive, gifted person' but he did all right. I don't know why my father thought it wouldn't suit him. I think it may have been because of my father's social standing; he felt that he could never rise socially in the Navy to the level that was

required. I think really he was 'passed over' (as they say); he didn't make promotion to Rear Admiral for no other than social reasons. You see, when you get to that level in the services, certain niceties are noticed. My father was the only man of his rank without 'private' means at all. He said that no-one reached that level in the Navy without actually being able to throw major parties which were not paid for out of their salary. I don't know if that was true or not but it all seems quite feasible.

"My family were quite musical. My father played the violin, but not terribly well. My mother played the piano and was very good indeed. And she was very fond of Glenn Miller. My father's father played the trumpet, and my paternal grandmother was the only one of the four grandparents who actually didn't play an instrument. My mother's father played all the reeds; literally all the reeds, clarinets, oboes and saxophones, and my mother's mother played the piano as well; she was quite good, too.

"My music started when I was at Portsmouth Grammar School. I remember being 14 when Lonnie Donegan's *Rock Island Line* was a hit and I was bought a guitar, and learnt 'the three chords'.... or, as Gary Glitter once said; 'E, A, and, er, erm....' But good old Lonnie! I vividly remember being taken to task after The Blues Band had done that South Bank Show on TV with Nine Below Zero and Dr. Feelgood. This chap asked me who I thought was really influential in the start of rhythm and blues in Britain and I said straight away – 'Lonnie Donegan – without a shadow of a doubt'. The following week in the *Melody Maker* they called me all kinds of things because I'd said that. 'Huh! What does he know.... he says Lonnie Donegan.... start of

Paul Jones and Fiona Hendley

the Blues.... etc etc....' But that is not what I meant. Lonnie made it possible. The three chords. And when he appeared on the radio, they asked him where he got all those songs from and he said 'Big Bill Broonzy – Leadbelly....' And off we all scooted, down to our record shops, looking for these records. Lonnie and Chris Barber, they started it. Barber brought over Broonzy, Muddy Waters, Sonny Boy Williamson, Sonny Terry & Brownie McGhee, Sister Rosetta Tharpe, all these crucial people. He brought the great harmonica player James Cotton to Britain – a big influence on Cyril Davies, moreso than Little Walter or Big Walter even; so let's not forget Lonnie, and especially his boss, Chris Barber.

"I started my collection of Blues records whilst I was at school. I was also buying jazz; King Oliver, Louis Armstrong, Jelly Roll Morton and especially Sydney Bechet. I particularly loved The Original Dixieland Jazz Band playing stuff like *Livery Stable Blues*. Then I saw *The Glenn Miller Story* and bought that album and Artie Shaw records, and of course, Humphrey Lyttleton. If you wanted to go and hear jazz being played, then it tended to be Humph, so I bought his records. I really loved clarinets so Artie Shaw was a real favourite. Clarinets and soprano saxophones; Goodman, Artie Shaw. One of my favourite tenor players was – and still is – Eddie 'Lockjaw' Davis. I remember some time later when I bought Count Basie's *Atomic Mr. Basie* album; Lockjaw had about four stunning solos on that album. He also did a lot of those trio albums with organ and drums; tenor sax, organ and drums! Those were the trios! *Jumping on Lennox, Beano* – which was a tribute to Coleman Hawkins.... I just loved all those saxophone things.

"I became known as P. P. Jones. Some of the books about the period get this wrong and they refer to me as P. P. Pond, which is ridiculous, because the second 'P' meant Paul *Pond* Jones. Also worth mentioning is the fact that the initials 'P. P.' did not stand for 'Permanently Pissed'; this was a story which has emanated from the Rolling Stones and is definitely untrue.

"Why Jones? It was because at one stage – I can't quite remember when – all pop stars had really silly names which real people simply wouldn't have, like Eden Kane and Billy Fury – things like that – and I didn't want to be called 'Adam Faith' or anything like that; I wanted to be called Smith or Jones. I

decided against Paul Smith but liked the ring of Paul Jones; it was just the most common name. Blues singers were called 'Jones'. 'Johnson' and 'Jackson' or 'King'; very basic, solid common names.

"At that time at Oxford my academic work was taking a back seat. I would sit up all night discussing say, T. S. Eliot, and then in the morning be completely unable to actually write anything about him. It was all rather silly. And half the reason I'd be up all night is that I'd been doing something else for the previous six nights and would suddenly discover that I had a paper to turn in. It was all rather silly, and very often I didn't turn in that paper because I felt dreadful; that Benzedrine is all right – keeps you going all night – but boy, you feel awful the following morning.

"The first harmonica player I ever heard was Sonny Terry. Sonny & Brownie were probably selling more records over in Great Britain than Broonzy, or on a level. But the first harmonica playing that 'shredded my head', so to speak, was by Junior Wells. My father was the Captain of Plymouth Dockyard when I was first at University in 1960. On my first vacation, I visited a shop in Plymouth, Pete Russell's Hot Record Store. I used to go in there and buy Mose Allison, Big Bill, Sonny & Brownie. One day, Pete Russell said to me 'You like Blues. Listen to this. What do you think?' And he played me this stuff.... it had this great, big, hard backbeat; a big, chunky piano and a fat bass.... and I thought what is *this*!? And then in came this wonderful, powerful rich and round electric guitar sound. I had never heard anything quite like it. I said 'what is *this*!?' He said 'T-Bone Walker'. I replied 'But.... but the man is a genius!' 'Yes,' said Pete, 'many people already know this – what's taken you so long?' It was a 10-inch LP on French Atlantic. Some of it was with a Chicago Blues band and on one track there was this harmonica – it was called *Play On Little Girl*.

"I had done one term at Oxford, but when I heard Junior Wells I thought.... *this* is what I want to do with the rest of my life....

"I went straight back to Oxford and tried to find some musicians. I went out and bought a harmonica. I don't know what I sounded like then, but it was Brian Jones who said to me one day 'You see that C harmonica there? If you actually play it in C you'll only ever sound like Jimmy Reed.'

Manfred and his men eat their way around Europe

"In those days, 'cross' harp was the thing; Brian said 'If you want to sound like Little Walter, then you have to take that C harp and play in the key of G on it.' Of course, since then, I've found that to be not exactly true; lots of harp players play it in the regular key – including Little Walter – and I do much of the time myself these days, just bending the notes where you can. You still get a great sound – it's the tone that matters. But then it was cross harp; by blowing, you'd only ever sound like Jimmy Reed. I was very grateful to Brian, because up until then I didn't really know. Brian was a very natural musician. He could pick up an instrument and get a tune from it. We did very briefly have a band together. Brian was living in Cheltenham and Alexis Korner had started playing with his band at the Ealing Club. I still lived in Oxford, and on his way every week to see Alexis, Brian would stop off at Oxford and stay overnight at my place. By this time I'd been sent down from University; it must have been late 1961 or the beginning of '62. There was always a party going on; if my band was playing at one, then Brian would often sit in with us. Although I'd left University, I still had contact with lots of students; some of my band were 'townies', but others were students. Anyway, Brian and I would hitch into Ealing to be at the Alexis gigs. We were just among the many young hopefuls and we would stand as close as we could to the stage because Alexis was very generous and would let the youngsters up to play. At this point Cyril Davies was in the band, I think Graham Bond was, Long John Baldry. All great musicians. But we'd all be stood around when Alexis was on; there'd be Art Woods, Mick and Keith, myself and Brian, many other hopefuls.

"It was probably something like a year before I became involved with Manfred Mann. I got a job as a dance band singer in Slough. I used to have to put on a red jacket with long lapels, one of those drapey things, with one link button, grease on my hair, and I had to do the current chart songs. I had to audition for that job. There were a hundred people turned up for that audition and 99 of them sang *The Young Ones*. I sang *I Can't Stop Loving You* or *Georgia on My Mind*. I think they were just sick of everyone doing a Cliff Richard song.

"The chart stuff at the time was all that Bobby Vee and Bobby Vinton stuff; *Roses are Red, my Love,*

Violets are Blue. As far as the British material, then apart from Cliff we had Adam Faith and Joe Brown; I remember having to sing *I Only Have A Picture of You*, which I didn't enjoy too much. The deal was, if I sang about five of those, they would let me sing a song of my choice. The band was trumpet, trombone, two saxes, rhythm section and there was a girl singer as well.

"They were called Gordon Reece and the Adelphians. He used to stand up at the piano and call out '91, 213 and 291' and they would all sift through their arrangements – they were all good readers. I'd be in the kitchen at the side of the stage drinking coffee and they'd open the door and call 'Paul!' and I'd be on. The manager didn't want me to be called Paul Jones. He thought it was a stupid name. But I protested 'Bluesmen always have names like "Jones"'. He said 'You're not a "bluesman" here! You're a dance band singer. You'll be called Paul Peterson!' There was already a Paul Peterson, an American recording artist who'd had a couple of hits, but there I was, Paul Peterson. At the same time I would be Paul Jones going off to Alexis's gigs.

"Cyril Davies had left Alexis by then and had formed his own band, the All Stars, which was in effect Screaming Lord Sutch's band; Carlo Little on Drums, Nicky Hopkins on piano, Cliff Barton on bass.... a great band.... Geoff Bradford on guitar. They used to play around places like Bushey and Harrow and I used to follow them around, get up and sing. I never really rated Cyril as a harp player but as a singer, yes; and that band was very powerful. There was a wrong story in circulation concerning Cyril Davies's death. It has been repeated in recent years, that he died from Leukæmia. Brian Knight, who was in Cyril's band, later married his widow. He said he didn't know how that Leukæmia story had started; 'Someone should have asked me', he said, 'I mean; I was there. All someone had to do was ask me, or Marie. Cyril didn't die of Leukæmia; he died from heart failure'.

"And so to the Manfreds. Mike Hugg, Mike Vickers and Manfred had been fired from Butlin's for their failure to 'play simply'. They were into jazz and moved to London. They refused to play rock, but rhythm and blues would be a good compromise. After all, Art Themen, Graham Bond and other great musicians were making a good living playing

Stompin' the Blues, 1991 (pic: Richard Austin)

rhythm and blues, so the precedent had been set. There was no 'shame' in playing R&B. So off they went to the Marquee, which in those days was the centre of rhythm and blues. Alexis had started a residency and again, I was always there. They asked Bill Carey, who used to MC there, if he knew of any unattached singers. He said 'Well, you might try this guy "Blue Boy Jones"' – that's what I was calling myself by then – I always wore denim, head to foot, 'he sometimes gets up with Alexis.' So they got my number from Alexis, phoned me and asked me to audition. I recall their so-called manager at the time saying on the phone, 'Do you know "Mannie Mann and Mike Hugg?" and I said "Is 'Mannie" Mann Manfred Mann who writes in *Jazz News*?' He said 'Yeah.... that's him'. I told him I didn't know him. He went on; 'Well, he's looking for a "shouter"'. Rather sniffily I replied 'Well I'm a singer....' He told me to go along for the audition and so I did. It was held at a Ska club in Carnaby Street called The Roaring Twenties. This was usually full of Jamaicans but at ten in the morning it was empty. And there was only me at the audition; I got the job. The line up of the band was Ian Fenby on trumpet, Tony Roberts, sax, Don Fay, Mike Hugg on drums, Manfred on Piano – this was before he'd bought his first organ – Dave Richmond on bass, Mike Vickers on sax.

"We had our first rehearsal in December 1962 in Manfred's flat in Forest Hill. It was snowing and I can remember Manfred sitting behind his piano in this cold room saying 'Y' know something man? We're gonna be bigger than The Shadows....' I thought, well; I hope we're not going to sound like the Shadows....

"So. We rehearsed away; very jazzy. Like Alexis Korner's band, we had this big Mingus thing going. But that was O.K. by me.

"During this time I still worked by day. The afore-mentioned Ben Palmer, the piano player, had got a job with Esquire records, which was a jazz label which did a certain amount of blues as well. They held the Prestige catalogue, so they carried all the Bluesville and Bluenote material. Not only did they do all the local stuff like Johnny Dankworth and

Ronnie Scott, they did all the great American material too; Miles Davis, the Modern Jazz Quartet – everything. I'd rang Ben one day and he'd put me onto this job which was going. They needed a travelling salesman to cover the London area. So I went to see this guy – Carlo Kramer. He told me it was no salary – just commission on sales. So I took it. There were no company cars in those days. I used feet and public transport, and my knowledge of London, which is legendary in some circles, stems from that era. I covered the whole of London from Cockfosters to Morden, from Heathrow to Loughton.

"We had some good blues on the labels. Eddie Boyd's *Five Long Years*, stuff like that. He had a label called Starlight which had done a deal with a label called Bandera, so he had people like Lonesome Jimmy Lee Robinson *All My Life* and Dusty Brown – people like that. Great little records. I used to traipse around London carrying all these records. However, by the end of March 1963 there was enough work for The Mann Hugg Blues

The Blues Band's first birthday at the Bridge House, 1980. Left to right: the late Ian Stewart, the late Alexis Korner, Hughie, Tom, Stevie Smith, Paul, Dave, Gary, Mike Vickers, Manfred Mann, Paul Gilleron

Brothers, as we had become known, to give up the day job.

"At about that time we played the Hanborough Tavern in Southall. A man came up to us and said 'I think I could do something for you boys on a management level.... my name is Ken Pitt'.

"So that would be sometime in the spring of 1963. We had various other horn players who came and went. I remember Alan Skidmore was playing tenor at one time. In the summer that year we auditioned for Decca, Pye and EMI. By then the the Beatles were happening, but not to the degree that Dick Rowe at Decca wasn't still turning down promising beat groups! We were turned down by both Decca and Pye. EMI accepted us. We recorded two unsuccessful singles; the instrumental, *Why Should We Not*, which featured sax and harmonica, and the second was a vocal called *Cock-a-Hoop*. The third single was commissioned by Rediffusion TV as the theme tune to a new series – *Ready, Steady Go!*. It was *54321*.

"I'm quite proud of that record, in a funny kind of way.

"What followed is fairly well known, but there are lies which are told about that period which I try to correct. The most persistent one concerns the origin of our repertoire as far as singles were concerned. The story goes around, and I don't know how this originated, but it is to be found even on the sleevenotes of the latest compilation of Manfred Mann, the EMI releases, that the repertoire was 'brought' to the group by our producer, John Burgess. This was not so.

"All those things like *Do Wah Diddy* and *Sha La La*, *Come Tomorrow* and *Oh No Not My Baby* - they were in my record collection. What used to happen was that I would listen avidly to any radio station which would play any kind of black popular music. Any station which would play blues, play soul or Motown. I just loved black pop music like The Shirelles, that kind of stuff. You might hear it on Radio Luxembourg, sometimes on the BBC.

"I used to go into Strickland's Record Shop in Dean Street, Soho, and say 'Look; these are the records I want this week'. And they would be stuff like *Night at Daddy Gees* by Curtis Lee and the All-Stars. It was just stuff which would never even get a sniff at the charts in Britain. *Do Wah Diddy*, for instance, was one of those. So I'd order these records and go back a week later to pick them up. I'd go home and listen to them and when the time came for rehearsals, to go into the studio or learn new material for the band, they'd say 'Any songs?' And I'd say 'Yes. I love this.... just listen....' And the first time John Burgess ever heard those songs is when I took them into him. He started bringing us some songs – *Pretty Flamingo*, for example, he brought us that.

"But I am very firm about the numbers he didn't bring us; I mean, how would anyone have known about *Come Tomorrow*, for example? I suddenly saw the name Marie Knight – I'd started collecting Gospel records by this time – she used to sing duets with Sister Rosetta Tharpe – *Up Above My Head I Hear Music in The Air* – from about 1950. But I saw this record listed in the music press of the day – Marie Knight singing *Nothing* – that was the 'A' side. Without hearing it I went to Strickland's and ordered it. Record shops were great in those days – obscure though it was, they got it. I brought it home, played it; the 'A' side was good, as I'd expected, a nice, beaty, up-tempo number. But.... when I flipped it over! As soon as I heard *Come Tomorrow* I said yes – that's the song I want to sing. I took it to the guys, we rehearsed it, recorded it: a hit.

THE SOLO YEARS

Being in Manfred Mann was never going to be my full career; it was always just going to be a part of it. It took me almost a year to leave the band, from handing in my notice to Mike D'Abo taking over. When I first gave notice, things were frosty. They said 'You can't leave. You have certain duties in a partnership like this'. But I went; I think it was about eleven months later. There were quite a few people up for my job; some of them quite famous, but I don't know much about it and I hate telling lies.

"But D'Abo was definitely the man for the job. By the time I was ready for going, and they'd got Mike, things were reasonably friendly. In fact, now they had somebody new, they were keen to have me leave so that they could get on with things. As soon as he realised I was to become solo, John Burgess said that I needed a manager. He got me Richard Armitage from Noel Gay.

"I'd been reading about this movie project of Peter Watkins for weeks. I'd read that it was going to

Harping on – Worthing, '92. (pic. Richard Austin)

star Eric Burdon. One day I got a call from Peter Watkins's office, saying would you like to be in a movie. My first reaction was that I didn't want a small part in an Eric Burdon movie, but they said no – he's not doing it; we're offering you the lead. So I met Peter Watkins who I really admired as he'd already made *The War Game* which, although no-one had seen it, was quite well-known as it had been banned by the BBC. Peter had also done a BBC TV movie which was very well done; violently realistic – *Culloden*. I thought the project he was offering me might be quite an interesting thing to be in. Up until this time, of course, although I had an interest in movies, I'd had no ideas or desire to be involved in acting. I got on extremely well with Peter. I liked him and I think he liked me. So I made *Privilege*. By today's production schedules, it was quite short in the making; about eight weeks. I think at the time I was pretty blasé about it all. 'Ho-hum.... it's The Movie now....' it was a change in lifestyle, getting up at five in the morning, etc. And I got on well with Jean Shrimpton.

"However, *Privilege*, as a movie wasn't followed by a flood of offers. Frankly, I just don't think I was good enough in it. And I remember I still had very bad skin and whenever directors would ask me to meetings for considering the 'good looking' parts, I wouldn't get the part. One American director once said to me 'Er.... that skin of yours is very marked.... does that show up on camera?' I said 'Well, I have to be honest – yes.' He just shook his head and said 'Er.... well.... I'm sorry....'

"The next major offer came again from Peter Watkins for a film called *Punishment Park*. He asked if I'd like to be in it. But at that time I rather naively said 'Look, Peter, I don't think I should make another "art" movie just now; I'd rather make a commercial movie and after that I'd be delighted to work with you again.' But the truth of the matter is I was never offered another decent part. I was offered some really daft, stupid things. Actually, I wasn't really good enough in *Privilege* to be offered anything decent. However, I did another movie, which was a small budget 'art' movie called *The Committee* which had music by Pink Floyd and The Crazy World of Arthur Brown.

"My solo career had not taken off as well as it could have done, although to be fair I did have some hits and I would have had more had it not been for the inefficiency of EMI. They were just so hopeless. I had a big record – *And The Sun will Shine* – written by the Bee Gees. This was selling six hundred copies a day and heading for the charts. It got into the top forty. I remember this so well. I was into the habit in those days of ringing the office and saying 'How many have we done?' This Monday morning I rang the office and asked how many we'd done up to the weekend and they said.... 'None'. Their explanation was that the shops had bought too many, so that by Friday, they had copies left and didn't order new stocks. Tuesday dawned, I rang again. How many did we sell? None. I said to my manager 'There has to be something wrong.' So he rang EMI and came back to me. 'You're not going to like this. It's not that there are no orders. There are no records.' They hadn't pressed any. I was angry; I told him to tell EMI to get some pressed. Later, he came back again. 'It seems worse than I thought. There are records.... but there are no labels....' Forty eight hours later, the record had died and fallen from the chart. Then EMI shipped the records. Too late.

They stiffed me, killed my record. I thought who needs a record company like this? In organisations that size, nobody notices a thing like that.

"Things moved on. I did a tour of New Zealand and Australia with The Who and The Small Faces. I was third on the bill. I had a very good little Australian band with a great Hammond organ player. I got on well with the other bands, and especially with Roger Daltrey. But I was far from being the classic 'rock & roll animal'; many of the backstage antics were foreign to me but they always had been. Even with Manfred Mann we used to be on tour with all these bands and we'd see all these things they got up to backstage and we still wouldn't be a part of it. We never were. I'm not going to paint us as angels, but that stuff didn't appeal. The Small Faces.... well; they were wild, but even some of them were quiet. Kenny Jones was a lovely, sweet guy and a tremendous musician.

"I came back from that tour and I thought 'I'm not cut out for a life like this....' A man called Charles Marowitz rang up and said he had a play going on at the Open Space Theatre – a tiny little fringe theatre – he said 'I'll be absolutely frank; I had an actor booked but he's landed a TV part in America. He's gone. I can't find an American actor. Now, you're a pop singer and you do American accents – will you come and audition?' I was ready for anything, I really was. The audition was the craziest thing. He said 'Do you know any speeches by heart?' I said I didn't. 'But you must know some songs by heart?' I said 'Of course.... what about *I've been a Bad, Bad Boy*?' He said 'Right. That is your text. This is real acting. You'll never get away with bogus acting with me. Acting is not pretending.' I said 'What is acting if it's not pretending?' He replied; 'Acting is being, but in a hypothetical situation – it's not pretending. Little children pretend. You've got the words of *Bad Bad Boy*- those are what you'll say; but your intention is to persuade some housewives in an Islington market to buy some canteens of cutlery. Now – go!'

"So I started to sell this cutlery with the text of *Bad Bad Boy*. I got through that, then he said 'You're a political activist on Hyde Park Corner. Use the same text to persuade all those listening to you in the crowd to follow you to the American Embassy in Grosvenor Square to hand in a petition to stop the war in Vietnam....' So I did, and he offered me the

job and I said 'Yes please.' I did a play called Muzeeka by John Guare who has recently had a success in the West End. Muzeeka had won an award off Broadway and I did it in this country with Connie Booth, who was not then Mrs. John Cleese. It was a fine company and my theatrical debut. Harold Hobson came to see it and gave me a sort of modest write up, but it was just enough to get me an audition for a play called *Conduct Unbecoming*. I got the job. We opened at the Bristol Old Vic, transferred to the Queen's Theatre in Shaftesbury Avenue, I played there for a year and then transferred to the Ethel Barrymore Theatre on Broadway.

"The world of the theatre was new and very exciting. Even movies hadn't excited me that much. Meeting Charles Marowitz was the turning point. He gave me books by Stanislavsky, Meyerhold and Grotowksy. It was terribly exciting. I remember when I was doing *Conduct Unbecoming* on Broadway and Grotowsky came to speak in New York. The meeting was in the Town Hall and was scheduled for midnight because that was the only time the actors and performers could get there. The place was packed and buzzing with all these actors and people from on and off Broadway. I even asked him a question myself, but I can't remember what it was. But he was one of the most powerful intellects I had ever come across.

"Although I was acting, there was still the music career. For instance, I was offered silly money – that means a lot – to tour Scandinavia in July of 1970. I said to my manager 'But – I'll be in New York with the play....' He said 'Here's the deal. You have to promise to do New York and they'll let you off a month early to tour Scandinavia.' So there I was – not saying 'I might' do New York, but actually promising to do it. So I got out of the London run a month early to tour Scandinavia. I think I was probably bigger in Scandinavia than anywhere else in the world, including Britain. On that tour we were playing for three weeks to between twelve and twenty thousand people a night. Mind you, it wasn't difficult getting audiences that size. It was in these huge open air 'Folk Parks' and there would be lots of people in there already, but the band was part of the attraction.

"Then I went over to New York. The play had had such good notices, especially the main review in The

It's a hard road: The original 1980 promotion shot

New York Times, that I decided to move over there lock, stock and barrel. Took the family, got the kids into school in New York, rented an apartment.

"Actually, the show didn't do as well as it had in London. It closed after six months and I found myself there with an apartment rented for a year. But I'd made a lot of contacts there because when I first went over I'd stayed in the Chelsea Hotel and seen all these people like Mike Bloomfield and others, and I used to frequent Fillmore East and when the English bands came over, like Humble Pie, Derek and The Dominoes, Pink Floyd, I was always there. At this point my manager said 'If you've got to live in America, why not make an album while you're there?' So that's when I made *Crucifix in a Horseshoe*. That's a strange album. It has some great musicians on it, though. People from Bob Dylan's band, Roberta Flack's band. It didn't do all that well. I loved working on that album. I used to go into the Brill Building and sit there with these guys like Archie Resnick and Rupert Holmes. Resnick wrote

Under The Boardwalk and Holmes wrote the *'Pina Colada Song'* much later but then we worked together on songs for my album. It got very good reviews in magazines like 'Cream' in America, but I think the record company didn't know what to do with it. They were expecting an album of *Pretty Flamingo* and *Bad Bad Boy*. But I did a follow up album to that which was never even released! That had great, great musicians on it. People like Gary Boyle, George Kahn on sax, Roy Babbington on bass, Dave McRea on keyboards. But it's all out there in the universe, somewhere, unreleased.

"Following this I made a terrible movie for Hammer. Great cast again – Robert Hardy, Michael Hordern, Patrick McGee. I also did a couple of TV plays, but basically I spent the rest of the 1970s in Repertory companies and touring theatrical productions. I did everything from *Hamlet* to *Joseph*. Edmund in *King Lear*. *Othello*. *Romeo & Juliet*. I'd done Shaw, Anouilh. All sorts of 'frightfully posh stuff....' And I did a lot of work in studios. At the time there was a big demand for harmonica playing on records. From country & western to straight pop. I also worked quite a lot for Andrew Lloyd Webber and Tim Rice. I did the *Evita* album – I played Eva's husband, Peron – and I played harp on just about everyone's record from Billy Connolly to Tina Turner, Tom Robinson, B. A. Robertson, Gene Pitney – everyone. It was due to playing on all those records, everything from techno-pop to country, and never blues, that I realised that I simply had to play blues again, and in a band.

"During the '70s I'd been plugging the gaps in my record collection, because in the latter half of the '60s I'd not bought what was coming out and missed a lot.

"I was playing Claudio in *Measure for Measure* at the Riverside Theatre with Helen Mirren and Michael Elphick. We used to have these musical evenings because two of the cast played guitars. I just couldn't stand it any longer; it was at that point that I rang Tom McGuinness.

THE TRUE STORY....

"I rang Tom because I couldn't think of anyone else. He was the first person who came to mind. I thought 'Who can I get together to play some Blues with?' I'd no idea what Tom was doing. I knew he'd parted company with Manfred ten years previously and I really hadn't kept contact since McGuinness Flint had finished. I said 'Are you up for it?' and he gave the famous reply 'Not if it's going to be six nights a week up and down motorways....' I replied that it would be one night a week, because I was already working six. And it would be in pubs, like the Hope & Anchor, The Bridge House, the Half Moon. I'd been to these places and mentioned to them that I was thinking of putting a blues band together and they would always come back with 'You've got a gig here anytime....' I dithered about it. I was in touch with Lew Lewis and his band – a great little Canvey Island outfit, much along the lines of Feelgood, but Lew was a much better harp player than Lee Brilleaux. I wondered for a while if I should get in touch with some of those guys. I'd spent so much time in the clubs in the late seventies that I knew just about everybody. That's why, when the Blues Band started, and occasions arose where not everyone was available for a gig, there was this floating population of players. I used to phone different guys

from all these outfits and say 'Can you gig with us?'

"Anyway, Tom got in touch with Hughie, and it was through the banjo player, Keith Nelson, that he'd heard about Dave being available. It was a stroke of luck Dave knowing Gary. And there were lots of people who were around at the beginning, too. Jo Ann Kelly appeared with us on many occasions; the late, great Ian Stewart, Lou Stonebridge.

The British Blues Connection presentation, 1993 (pic: Mark Brooklyn)

Tom and I wanted the musical format to be right, too. It wasn't to be twenty minutes solos and jams. We worked out arrangements, it was entertaining and we would write too. I think the whole thing took us by surprise. I recall that gig where we drove to High Wycombe to the Nag's Head and the promoter had the Merton Parkas booked. It was then that The Blues Band became 'professional' and really ceased being a 'pub' band. The rest, as they say.... is history. The future? I like the Blues Band, we enjoy what we do. I think it's terrific that we can just go on playing."

The very first big tour – 1980s 'Spring Cruise': here the Blues Band and the Dance Band join forces for combined mugshots with manager Ray Williams ('twixt the beard and moustache)

"How's my Son Rob Doing?"

The Hughie Flint Story

While southern boys were hunting down their Howlin' Wolf or rocking at the Ealing Club, way up north, in Manchester, a noble and ancient blues oracle held court in a youth club. There, young would-be musicians would hear of new and exotic music. The oracle's name was John Mayall, and his most promising acolyte was a young drummer who would hump his kit onto the bus every week to sit at the feet of the Master. Hughie Flint was born in Manchester in 1943. He was the Blues Band's first drummer, and left in 1981 because of the pressures of touring. He was replaced by his good friend, Rob Townsend, with whom he claims to have a 'Father and Son' relationship. Hughie Flint is a key figure in the development of British blues music. During his three years with John Mayall, The Bluesbreakers had a cavalcade of guitar stars passing through their ranks. John McVie and Peter Green, both of Fleetwood Mac, Mick Taylor, who joined the Rolling Stones, and of course Eric Clapton. Hughie went on to further fame with Georgie Fame & The Blue Flames, Alan Price, and eventually the chart topping McGuinness Flint. Like his 'son', Rob, Hughie never wanted to be a rock'n'roller. It had to be jazz. Today he lives a quiet life in a peaceful Oxfordshire village. Apart from the occasional Irish music session, when he'll play boudrahn, Hughie Flint has put the hectic world of music behind him, devoting most of his time to his Buddhist meditation and his job at Oxford University. Tom McGuinness finds it hard to understand why his old partner should ever want to give up playing. Yet Hughie Flint is contentment itself, which is quite an achievement if you look at where he's been.

"When I was two, I grabbed this tin drum that my Auntie had. I began to play it so she actually gave it to me. I was allowed to take it home and it probably drove everyone mad. At the age of about five, six and seven, I used to lay out books around me, as if they were drums, and my mother would open a drawer in the sideboard and suspend a saucepan lid from it as if it were a cymbal. I would then play this 'drumkit' along to whatever was on the radio – every day. Until, by the time I was nine, they'd bought me a bass drum, snare, etc., so that by the time I was 12 I had the full kit. By the time I was 14 I was an avid radio listener, mainly jazz. Jack Parnell, Kenny Baker, Humphrey Lyttleton, all those people. But what really knocked me out was seeing Louis Armstrong in The Glenn Miller Story. Not only did that movie have Armstrong's trumpet, but it had Gene Krupa and Cozy Cole. This was real, real Jazz, for the first time. Very soon I realised that Louis Armstrong was not alone – there were others: Fats Waller, Lionel Hampton. These records were a revelation.

"When I reached 16 I was, by this time, totally crazy about jazz. It was a time when the Musicians' Union came to the end of its ban on American musicians visiting here, so in succession, I managed to get to see Armstrong, Sydney Bechet, Duke Ellington, Count Basie, Lionel Hampton – the lot.

"Having John Mayall, who is of course ten years older, as your Youth Club Leader, was quite unique. I was about seventeen at this time and we'd go to the club and all be exchanging ideas about jazz. By the time I was 19 or 20 I was visiting John at his house. He had this vast array of material from field recordings of work hollers through to Ornette Coleman and everything in between. I now heard even more inspirational drumming. Elvin Jones, Max Roach. These were, and still are, my heroes.

"It was John Mayall who introduced me to the blues. I wasn't as interested as I was in jazz, but I did find it fascinating. John at this time was married, with a family, and working in Manchester as a graphic artist. His house was a treasure trove of recordings; shelves were lined with reel-to-reel tapes of recordings he'd make nearly every night; he'd miss nothing; American Forces Network, (AFN), Luxembourg; in fact anything that might play blues or jazz.

"John knew it was what he wanted to play, and the plan was that he'd move down to London, get a new job and form a band. I'd be the drummer and once he'd got settled, he'd call me down from Manchester. By now I'd got married. John moved to London and we moved into his house in Manchester. Eventually, the call came. It was the end of 1963 when I moved to London. John had a band together, already with a drummer, but the drummer had a day job. I got a day job in a factory in Catford. John's band were good and had no trouble signing with the Rik Gunnell Agency. Soon they were getting bookings. Once John had reached the average of five gigs per week, he said to me 'Are you ready to join?'

"The line up was John McVie, bass, Bernie Watson, who was quite a good guitar player but played with his back to the audience, John and me. Bernie Watson left the line up soon after. I don't know what happened to him. We picked up Roger Dean in his place. It was now Spring, 1964. The Bluesbreakers did mainly traditional, urban type blues, but John very soon began to write.

"We'd got this deal with Decca and the live album *John Mayall plays John Mayall* was recorded in a very unusual way. Klooks Kleek Club was in the Railway Hotel, West Hampstead, and right next door to the Decca Studios. Decca just ran mike cables from the studio, over the roof and into the pub and recorded the gig live. Primitive, but quick.

"Everyone now knows about the succession of guitarists who passed through The Bluesbreakers. When Eric Clapton came into the line-up in early '65 the band was totally transformed both music-wise and gig-wise. Rik Gunnell realised what a draw Eric was. There are always grey areas when recalling that period. It was an exciting time, and things moved fast. I know that everyone says that whilst Eric was away from the band for about four months, Peter Green stepped in straight away. I seem to recall we had a guitar player for a while called Geoff Cribbet, then Peter Green. But it's documented that Peter Green was there. We tried out so many guitarists during that period. They actually used to come along to gigs and step in with the band; God knows

what the audiences used to think. During that gap when Eric was away John sacked John McVie and got in Jack Bruce. That was amazing because I knew what a good player was and when Eric came back, it was electric; that first gig together they just gelled immediately. Dynamic though Jack was, he didn't remain too long, because he was lured into Manfred Mann's band.

"Touring in those days was a rigourous experience. Although I never went abroad with The Bluesbreakers, we certainly clocked up the miles just in the UK. It seems hard to believe now, yet wherever we played we very rarely stayed overnight. We had a Commer van and John, always the practical man, had built two bunks in the back which we used to take turns in whilst travelling. There'd be all the equipment crammed around us, one passenger seat and the engine cover, which occasionally one of us would have to sit on. Claustrophobia, paranoia; you name it. John would get up onto the top bunk and go to sleep, someone would take their turn in the passenger seat. The Gunnel Agency had a random attitude to booking gigs. We'd be in Bournemouth one night then Newcastle the next.

On each occasion we would drive back to London. There was a rota system for who got the passenger seat. To be honest, I hated all that. Only rarely would we stay at extremely grotty bed & breakfasts. John was in charge of all the management and financial arrangements with the band, and he ran a very tight ship. It was his attention to such detail which kept us on the road and has kept him reasonably successful since. We were paid fifteen quid a week. John was shrewd and tight. At gigs, he'd stand at the door with this numbering-clicker device and diligently count the punters as they came in. He'd be there right up until we were just about due to go on.

"There was no chance ever of a promoter ripping The Bluesbreakers off. That kind of precedent was set by John and it's served him well to this day. He would pay us, then any expenses, then the petrol. The money fluctuated quite a lot, as even when Eric was with us, the fortunes of the band went up and down. But I now know that the band earned a lot more money than the proportional payments we were earning.

"Several weeks after Eric had left, I played my last gig with John at the Marquee. Peter Green was with us by then. My replacement, incidentally, was to be Aynsley Dunbar. Anyway, at the time of me leaving our band wages were thirty quid a week. That night, John came up to me and gave me twenty five pounds. 'Sorry, Hughie, we've not been doing so well since Eric left so it's only twenty five. Good luck and thanks for all your work with the band....' I remember being a bit puzzled by that, because although Eric had gone Peter Green was quite an attraction and here was the Marquee, absolutely heaving. So I turned around and Alexis Korner was standing there. He said 'Would you be interested in playing in my band?' So I did.

"However, some years later, John played the Albert Hall and I visited the gig with his ex-wife. Afterwards, John said 'We're off to the Speakeasy now – you coming?' I told him I was a bit tight for cash. 'That's all right,' he said, 'I can lend you some money'. So I asked him for the loan of a fiver. We arrived at The Speakeasy and I never spent the fiver. I never paid him it back, either, because I always considered that to be the fiver he owed me from that last gig at the Marquee!

"I can't quite remember when I met Tom McGuinness, but I know for a fact that he came

along with Manfred to several Mayall gigs. It was when Eric was with the band and as Eric was a friend of Tom's I got to meet him. Of course, the Manfreds had been having hits and I was quite aware of who they were. I'd met up with quite a few people. Ian Stewart, for instance, the Stone's piano player. I'd gigged with The Rolling Stones – the first one was a May Ball at Oxford University. They actually flew back from the States for that one; they'd committed themselves by contract. It was then that I struck up my friendship with Ian, which lasted right up until his death. I chatted with the others, and often would meet Charlie Watts in Footes, the drum shop, and we'd talk drums and he'd be grumbling 'Oh, I need to get heavier sticks....' They'd often turn up at our gigs. I liked the Stones, but they were not such a great personal influence. By the mid-60s I was much more of a Beatles fan.

"I'd been with The Bluesbreakers for quite some time and was tired of being constantly on the road. Then there was the changes in the band and of course, Eric's final departure, which wasn't all that graceful, because he'd formed Cream with Ginger and Jack without John's knowledge. When Peter Green came in, I just thought that with him and John McVie it simply wasn't the same. I was unhappy, and I kept telling John that 'I might be leaving soon....' John soon found another drummer, and telephoned me to tell me that the Marquee would be the last gig. I was fortunate that Alexis Korner had asked me to play for him. So there were three people John Mayall 'sacked': John McVie, Eric and me.

"I enjoyed playing with Alexis, and after some time I had a phone call one day from Georgie Fame. He asked me if I'd do a session for him; it was a single entitled *Because I love You*. It was released after he'd had the hit with *Yeh Yeh* but unfortunately it didn't do all that well. After the session, Georgie asked me if I wanted to join his band. I was attracted to the idea but I was trying to get our bass player, Binkie McKenzie, into the band as well – he was an amazing player. But Georgie said he was happy with Rick Brown.

"I lost touch with Binkie and sadly I learned later that he'd gone mad. I was approached only recently by an American musicologist who was doing a thesis for a Californian University on '60's English music – amazing how you can get a grant there to do something like that – he knew of Binkie. Binkie was another Jack Bruce – but I learned from this American that he had a brother called Bunny McKenzie who was a guitarist. The level of detail these researchers come up with is staggering. But poor old Binkie; he simply vanished off the scene.

"Alexis took it badly that we were trying to leave, but sadly Alexis's band wasn't particularly going anywhere. Alexis was a similar band manager to John Mayall, although he was a bit looser and relaxed about it. The trouble was I was married with a child and the money did figure. Although there was a good angle with Alexis; the chemistry was better and he allowed musicians more head, but a fiver here and seven quid there wasn't as attractive as the prospect of working with Georgie. However, Georgie's band turned out to be a bit more sophisticated and I was quite a rough and ready kind of R&B player. He had this big horn section, for instance – at times it was almost like playing with Count Basie. I didn't get on with the bass player, we had different attitudes to the music and after six months we came to a mutual agreement and I left.

"From the latter part of 1968 and into 1969 I didn't work all that much. I played the odd gig here and there and I played with Manfred Mann; the band was coming to the end of its natural life, and I

simply played percussion, congas, maraccas, stuff like that. In fact I played on their very last gig. Then I was offered a job with Alan Price's band.

"Like Georgie Fame, Alan's career had moved into the wider field by now; it was the big variety clubs like Batley, Stockton and Darlington. I didn't do any recording with Alan, but we did a few TV shows. It wasn't long before I moved on.

"Tom McGuinness and I met up and we had a mutual liking for Bob Dylan's group, The Band. The Band were all about family and community, they had this backwoodsman image; musicians playing on porches and in bars. Tom had had this clean-cut pop star image to maintain during his Manfred years and I'd attempted to keep up the look of a jazzman. But although it was a little late in the decade, we grew our hair. I had actually been approached by Manfred when his band folded. He asked me if I wanted to form a new band with him but I wasn't keen on playing Manfred Mann-style music. However, he assured me it was going to be a more experimental and more rock orientated. I was vaguely interested. Mike Hugg wanted to switch from drums to keyboards. We did actually have a couple of rehearsals but nothing came of it.

"And so, with Tom, McGuinness Flint was formed. It was a very exciting time for us, especially

Hughie at Mrs Flynn's in Ireland, 1971. L-R: Mrs Flynn, Tom, Paul Gilieron, Hughie, Dennis Coulson.

when a friend of Tom's introduced us to Benny Gallagher and Graham Lyle. They were such good writers and performers. We rehearsed that band for a whole year. When it 'happened' I was very intrigued with the notion of being a 'pop' star. And we had Glyn Johns as a producer. But it seemed very quickly over. Once we'd got the singles and the album out, we did TV and then began touring. We didn't seem to have done all that many gigs before Graham and Benny decided they wanted to leave, and it appeared that all that work simply went down the pan. One of the problems was that we'd rehearsed for so long, gone into the studio and made a very successful album with a top-notch producer, gone straight into the charts and when we were suddenly thrown onto the road we realised we simply weren't very experienced at playing together in a live situation. Now that sounds like a contradiction, but the stage is a totally different thing to being couped up in a studio or a rehearsal room. Our singer, Dennis Coulson, was very undisciplined on stage. There we were, having to live up to this hit single and Graham and Benny knew that the band wasn't really working out. They felt they were in the wrong band, and thought they'd be better off going their own way as a duo as they'd had the initial exposure. They had such a huge amount of material, too.

"We were devastated by their departure, but we picked ourselves up and decided we should re-form, and try to make it more of a gigging band rather than just a recording and rehearsal band. So we got Neil Innes, John Bailey on guitar and Dixie Dean on bass. We went to Ireland to rehearse, spent a month in Cork. We had an agency, went on the road, but soon it began to fall apart again. Neil Innes didn't get on with John Bailey, John left, we carried on with Neil for a while but McGuinness Flint, apart from those two hit singles, didn't really work. We reformed yet again, this time with Lou Stonebridge. Dixie and Jim Evans, on guitar. But it never took off. The albums bombed, we went from label to label, we gigged quite a lot, went to Germany, and generally staggered along, but there was one particularly bright spot during this period. We recorded an album of Bob Dylan songs, called *Lo and Behold*. It got a superb review in *Rolling Stone* and I'm told on good authority that when they played the album to Bob Dylan, he said it was the best performances of his material he'd ever heard. Strangely, it never took

Would-be jazzman Flint with The Bluesbreakers 1966: (Pic: Decca Records)

off here, but it was a particularly good album.

"McGuinness Flint carried on sporadically until early 1975 when I was hospitalised with a collapsed lung. I was quite ill for a time. The band folded.

"When I recovered, I did something I've done periodically throughout my career. I took a day job. I became a postman in Lewisham. I lived in Blackheath, so it was handy. Tom and I still put the odd band together, did charity things and assorted gigs like The Albany in Deptford. I just felt at that time as I have done in recent times, that I'd been on the road for so long, spent so much time in music that I wanted a break, a more simple lifestyle. I've always had that conflict, a pull in two directions – a love of playing music yet a desire for a slightly more stable existence. This took me up to '76, when I stopped being a postman to join Ronnie Lane's band. This was just for a tour, supporting Eric Clapton's band. Ronnie had just had success with Slim Chance and I knew Ronnie's music from the Faces. He'd had a lay-off, too, so we were enjoying the prospect. We got a nice band together; Ian Stewart, Charlie Hart and others and we flew to Copenhagen. The tour was to span about two months, and the travel arrangements were great. From Copenhagen we travelled all the way through Europe by train, including the Orient Express with the dining car, the sleeper car.

"At each town we stopped at we'd play a gig, all the way down to Munich. Supporting Eric's band was great; when Eric came on at the end doing something like *Goodnight Irene* we'd all be there; there was a great cameraderie, but it soon seemed to be over. There was a Mediterranean cruise follow-

Hughie with German fans – The Sisters Blusch, 1980

ing that and we did gigs in Ibiza and one in Barcelona. It was all rather nice.

"This was 1977 and around that time I'd begun toying with Irish music. I played the boudrahn with a traditional Anglo-Irish band, Chanter for about the next two years. That was virtually all the music I played in that period running up to the formation of The Blues Band. I got a call from Tom, or should I say I think it was Tom, I can't quite remember, and I recall we turned up for a rehearsal at a warehouse in Deptford. Before this I'd got together with Tom to discuss the idea of the band. It was to play the music we all loved but had been sidetracked from. To be honest, I'd never regarded myself as a blues musician, yet it was what everyone regarded me as. We were going to play good arrangements, there'd be no extended jamming.

"When we got together I didn't know Gary, and I'd only know of Dave rather vaguely, although I knew his sister Jo Ann quite well. Really it was my first meeting with Dave. I couldn't remember the John Dummer band at all, although it is possible that I'd met Dave somewhere in the past. I was actually on the dole when we got together. I got the impression that Gary was a bit awed by it all; after all, he was really the baby of the band and out of us the one who was least sure of himself, although that

soon altered. We rehearsed well, so that by the time we played the first gig at the Bridge House in April '79 we'd really got it right. I have a tape of us playing at The Pegasus, which is now closed, and we sounded pretty good, as we'd got all the arrangements and it was all very co-operative and democratic. Even Gary, who was very tentative at first, had begun to contribute, and there was no real band leader, we all contributed.

"Of course, we all knew what a draw Paul was, and we appreciated that. People knew us in some rough order, Paul first, Tom, probably Dave and then Gary and I, but we insisted eventually that if the band were advertised they'd never be 'Paul Jones and his Blues Band'; it was democracy and this 'no leader' thing was good for us. Of course, the media and TV wanted it differently. The Blues Band was a culmination of my career to date.

"I suppose I'd realised early on that I wouldn't make a jazz drummer. I'd taken my technique up to a certain point but that was when I was emulating Art Blakey and Elvin Jones back in the Manchester days. I realised that I was just an average jazz drummer. When I was playing with John Mayall I was forced to lock into this more simple way of playing, and I was influenced then by Ginger Baker. Not that I tried to play like Ginger, but I'd seen him play jazz with Graham Bond years before so to me it was an incredible way of playing. There was no such term then as a 'rock' drummer; you were simply a drummer playing jazz or rhythm and blues. You can hear my style for instance on the Klooks Kleek album where I'm a lot more jazzy and fussy than on the later recordings with John Mayall where I'm playing this simpler, rooted down style. My style just became more simplified and less technical over the years.

"Having said that, when I left The Blues Band, I did play for a while with Jimmy Jewel's band, the sax player who was at one time with McGuinness Flint and that was a very straightforward post-bop band. I have a tape we did with them. Jimmy played a great tenor and composed all the tunes. It was piano, bass and drums, a good line up. We did our own recording actually at a studio that Gary was involved with, but it was just an album we sold at gigs, not generally distributed. So in some way I went back full circle.

"I don't regret any of The Blues Band years, but I left because I'd stopped enjoying it. That last year I hardly saw my wife and I thought the Band had moved away from what I thought it was about. Material wise and show wise we'd wandered away somehow. Everyone was writing songs, and I didn't think a lot of them were that great. We'd become a well-rehearsed show, and a lot of the standards we'd played originally had become sidelined. I felt that the stuff we were writing wasn't as good as that stuff, the Muddy Waters material, etc. Plus there was a lot of conflict within the band.

"We'd peaked in late 1980; we were just huge everywhere but the last album I was involved with, Itchy Feet, I wasn't very pleased with. After that peak we started doing the circuit again, but this time to smaller audiences. The band seemed to be in

decline, and I decided to cut my losses. However, contrary to what some journalist wrote, I didn't leave the band in the middle of a tour. I'd said I was going at Christmas, I told them this in September; I said I'd do the Christmas shows and then finish. In the meantime they found Rob, and my leaving was in fact quite amicable.

"There were many times after two hard years of living in each other's pockets when we really began to get on each other's nerves. For instance, we were still sharing hotel rooms up until mid to late 1980; you just couldn't get away from each other, and it was such a relief when we finally began booking single rooms. I could actually do some meditating at last!

"The future? I've got my job at the University, I'm happy here with Fran, I've got a grandchild, my kids come and see me, I'm happy now. I buy lots of jazz re-issues and blues stuff. I played a gig here in the local pub recently, it was fine, but I wouldn't like to take it further than that. My son's in a band, playing drums, my daughter's in a band, I'm still very much into music in many ways. But being in a band is a commitment. I always liked to get into a band, get things as well rehearsed as possible then take it out on the road. I've always met people and that has happened.

"But after going to India, I came back and decided I would not play, and since then I've not met anyone and it's not happened, so I feel in a way that it's right. I did a few gigs with The Blues Band, with Rob, during 1987-88, but I told them that I was going to Nepal, with a specific purpose to further my Buddhist practice, and that when I returned I wouldn't be playing again. So there it is. All that remains to be said is that I enjoyed The Blues Band; it was a good time, the apex of my musical career."

Old originals: John Spence, Lari Myakicheff and seasoned campaigner Chris Runciman, await the return of Big Pete Turner from the pub

Pride of place: Lari tends his flock in the studio, early '80s

Unsung Heroes

Roadies

When what we now know as 'the rock band' began in the late 1950s, amplifiers were the size of a small suit case and many guitars, being basic models, were a handy item in a soft plaid or oilcloth case. As long as your singer was willing to help the drummer, you could travel to most gigs on the bus.

Most venues, pubs and clubs, had their own 'Tannoy' system; the term 'PA', for 'Public Address' was not in general use then. There would be a dodgy piano, a small stage. Apart from the odd spotlamp, lighting rigs were unheard of, unless you were lucky enough to be playing Butlin's or the Mecca chain of ballrooms. Dressing rooms were for theatre people; musicians usually had to crowd into evil smelling little kitchenettes at the side of the stage, or very often tune up in some dark corridor (some things never change). The only concession to 'stagecraft' might have been strips of multi-coloured foil as a backdrop for the drummer. Drum kits were basic, too; a snare, a tom-tom, hi-hat, cymbals and that awkward piece of baggage, a bass drum. Most of the very early groups often played without a bass player.

The Fender bass guitar was virtually unknown outside of London in the late '50s, and to young rockers, unless you were very lucky to know someone who played it, the upright string bass was a mysterious brown giant only seen in movies or on television. The total power output of a pub group in 1960 might only have been 50 watts. Compared with today's output at a medium size venue – anything from 5000 watts upwards, it seems a wonder to our modern jaded ears that we were ever able to listen to anything and become excited. If you compare even the Beatles' backline at Shea Stadium, with their state-of-the art Vox equipment, to the 18 38-ton pantechnicons used by Dire Straits and The Blues Band on the '92 European Tour, you'll begin to realise that the musicians we flock to see are only the cherry on a very heavy, complex cake. The term 'Roadie' has a long history. In the old days there was 'The Manager' – he was the man back in town with the leather-topped desk and the big cigar. On tour, a new position developed – that of the Road Manager.

He got you there, made sure you got paid, sorted out dragon landladies and generally kept the show on the road. The term became abbreviated to 'Roadie'. Today different bands of different sizes have different levels of management still, but since the growth in both the power and size of amplification equipment, the term roadie is more likely to apply to the roustabout; a tough, no-nonsense individual who can lift, fetch and carry.

Anything connected with Rock & Roll touring has its modicum of glamour. It is often the case that roadies are caricatured as thick, baseball-capped humpers with a vocabulary which goes something like "One-two.... One-two!" But a roadie's life is one of the hardest, most responsible jobs in the music business. The level of electrical knowledge alone can be staggering. The sheer drudgery of setting-up and taking down, night after night after night is not for the squeamish. As musicians become more famous, they can afford better roadcrews, and be more demanding. A good roadie knows exactly where to stand the guitars, how to tune them up, what levels to set the amplifiers at, what each band member drinks on stage, and how much. He's a mechanic, an electrician; often a musician. He has to have a sense of stagecraft and needs to be able to adjust the sound of the show to fit a dozen different venues. At the end of the show, the audience applaud their heroes. The lights dim, the band go backstage for food, drinks and fan adulation. The roadie works, dismantling the whole rig, packing it with a jigsaw precision into trucks. Often, as the band hit their hotel beds in the afterglow of another fine gig, the roadcrew are off, driving through the night to the next distant town, ready to do it all again. A good band keeps a good roadcrew. One man has been with them from the start.

"Voyage not completed"

The Lari Myakicheff Story

Lari Myakicheff was born in East Dulwich, South London, in 1946. Long before his association with The Blues Band he was working with Dave Kelly's band, The Dogs, during the 1970s. His father was a Russian emigré who left his offspring for Canada whilst Lari was still a babe in arms. He has not been heard from since.

Lari is the eldest of four children. He has three sisters. One works in Ulverston, Cumbria, for the local council. One works in North London, where she designs gardens. The other, his half-sister from his mother's second marriage, recently left Art School. Lari's early experience upon leaving school, when he spent six months as an apprentice electrician stood him in good stead in later life. With his wife, Nicky Myakicheff, who now runs The Blues Band's merchandising operation at most gigs, Lari has become as much a part of The Blues Band as any of the musicians. Since the early days at The Bridge House, right through to the massive Dire Straits Tour, Lari has lovingly handled the stage management, the backline, every bottle of Perrier water, and knows every intricate musical quirk the band may desire. He still lives in the area where he was born. This is his story:

"I went to school just down the road from here. I wasn't very good at school. I was very interested in something the school didn't do; art, sculpture, stuff like that. But there was no Art class at our school. The nearest I could get was technical drawing, so I threw myself into that. The last I saw of my father was before I was about six years old. He went off to Canada, and was last heard of in New York. I've never heard from him. He may still be alive; I don't know.

"When I left school I went to evening classes to do fine art and sculpture. But I only had one 'O' level in technical drawing. The first job I had when I left school was as an apprentice electrician. After just under or over a year of that, I went into the Merchant Navy. That would have been in early 1963. Just before that they sent me to the Merchant Navy Training vessel the *Vindicatrix* at Sharpness. I was trained for ten weeks to become a deckhand. It was a terrible winter; the snowdrifts were much taller than me.

"My first ship was the *Port MacQuarie*. We sailed to Buenos Aires. I had a bad experience on that trip. I recall going ashore with the crew, all the 'ABs', the older blokes. We cruised all the bars, as we did in those days. Trouble was, I didn't know when to stop. I recall walking back to the docks, then everything going blank. When I woke up, I was down a hole in some roadworks. I'd fallen down a trench and passed out. I was covered head to foot in mud. I managed to stagger back to the ship, saw the doctor straight away. I was so ill. He told me I was suffering from alcoholic poisoning and pumped me full of drugs. I couldn't do anything for a week. There was no sympathy at all from the bosun. There never was. But it taught me a valuable lesson. I've only been a moderate drinker since then. I did a couple of trips down South America way, and then went to Canada on the *Beaverfir*. Nova Scotia, places like that. There was Holland, the German ports, the Mediterranean. A bit of everything, really. Then I suddenly took a liking to Jersey. I jumped ship there in the summer of '64. I went to a farm and asked for a job. Surprisingly, they gave me one, and I spent several enjoyable months there. Then the law caught up with me and I was deported. I came back to England. I did a bit of building work and then got into tree felling. That was interesting. But this was long before I had anything to do with the music business.

'IT WAS EASY THEN....'

"I remember one night sitting around with friends saying 'Wouldn't it be nice to go to

59

Afghanistan, smoke an awful lot of dope, then come home....' So we thought; Yes. Let's do it. So we saved a little money, I managed to put together about 180 quid, which, looking back was quite a lot. I thought we'd go out there for a couple of months then come home. In fact I ended up being away for over two years. I managed to get hold of some Student Union Travelcards – illicitly – we all bought train tickets to Thessaloniki in Greece. From there we hitch-hiked into Istanbul where we hoped to get our visas for Iran and Afghanistan. As it turned out, we weren't able to do that.

"The Shah was still in power then, and the Iranians were celebrating 3000 years of Persian monarchy. They were very sensitive about travellers at the time and they shut the borders for a month. So there we were, stuck in Istanbul. It wasn't too bad. There was four of us and we still had some money. We lived cheaply in small rooms. Myself, my girlfriend and another couple. The other couple, incidentally, ended up in Australia, and they settled there. To the best of my knowledge, they're there today.

"We looked at the map and thought we'd take a different route. It seemed simple; nip up into the USSR, then down through Samarkand, then to Afghanistan. Naively we all went off to the Russian embassy. They laughed us out of the building. So we got a flight down to Tel Aviv and worked on a Kibbutz for a time. I ended up staying there for six months. It was easy then. I found Israel very interesting, especially from the historical aspect.

"It was a great place to travel around in. I saw all the sights, visited all the Holy places. I ended up doing construction work at Eilat on the Red Sea. So there's buildings down there with a bit of me in them. I used to look down at Eilat from the hills where I'd built a hut out of driftwood. There was a mixed community of international workers. There was quite a little shanty town which had built up there. Nobody minded me building my hut in the hills. But the time came to move on. And there were difficulties.

"If you'd stayed in Israel for over three months, an entry was made in your passport which meant you were unable to go to any Arab countries. Being surrounded by Arab countries, this made things rather awkward. So, we decided to take a ferry over to Cyprus. Once in Cyprus we could go to the British Consulate and exchange our passports for a new, clean one. Which is what we did. We then flew into Beirut. Beirut then was a thriving, cosmopolitan city. Once there I got talking to some American students who were attending the American university there. They found us a bed in the dormitory which was very helpful for a few weeks. After that we moved up into the mountains. During all this trekking I kept my mother supplied with postcards, although I never managed to get home. It was all too much of an adventure.

"Although I'd saved up some money whilst in Israel, I was beginning to run out of funds. I'd now been almost a year on the road. Eventually the group I'd set out with from England fell apart. We went our different ways, quite amicably. I was headed for India. Eventually I arrived in Old Delhi. I was almost broke and I remember wandering around Delhi railway station. I couldn't possibly afford any accommodation, even at Indian rates. I went up this flight of stairs at the station and saw this window at the top. It looked out on a kind of balcony which was built over the station facade. I thought it looked like a nice place to sleep that night. I ended up staying there for over three weeks. No-one bothered me. It was quite nice.

"I met up with an American guy. We travelled together for a while. But alone, I eventually arrived in Afghanistan. By now I was travelling with a primus stove and cooking pots. I existed on fruit and vegetables from local markets. Once I arrived in Afghanistan, it was everything and more than I'd expected. the people were warm and friendly, very generous. In India, kind though they were, there seemed to be too many people. There was this huge throng of humanity crowding around all the time; I couldn't handle it. They all wanted desperately to try out their English on you. But in Afghanistan it was different. My fondest memory is on reaching the lakes at Band-I-Amir, east of Kabul in the foothills of the Hindu Kush. I was making my living on my wits alone by then. I loved Afghanistan. Yet I kept travelling. I moved through the Khyber Pass and into Pakistan but I wasn't too keen. Back in India again, I felt that sheer weight of humanity bearing down. So I made a break for the border and ended up in Nepal. It was like a breath of fresh air. I managed to find some space again. I went up to Khatmandu where I stayed for a month. The break did me good, because when I eventually did move back into India I found I could handle it better. In Nepal I rented a room. The people were absolutely wonderful there. I saw some magnificent sights. the mountains, the valleys.... staggering.

"After Nepal, back in India, I gravitated towards Bombay. I wandered right down the West Coast. At one point I ended up in Rishikesh where I studied meditation for a while. That's the place the Beatles had visited. The whole town was vegetarian. There was no meat allowed there. There was a big Buddhist community formed from the Tibetans who had been forced to flee across the Himalayas. In southern India, I'd attempted to get a visa for Ceylon. I failed because they didn't want itinerant travellers, especially those with no money.

"I just kept on travelling, but eventually I had to make a decision. I had about three pound's worth of rupees left. I knew it was just about time to think of going home. I got in touch with a friend in London and he sent me out twenty five pounds. I thought I'd take my chances and see how far I could get on that. In fact, I got as far as Istanbul. It was a journey of local buses, hitch hiking, whatever I could manage. When I got to Istanbul, I was absolutely broke.

"I hadn't eaten for two days. I carried on and eventually arrived in Thessaloniki in Greece, where the whole adventure had begun. I was absolutely starving. I gave in and thought 'That's it. I'm going to the British Consulate; they'll re-patriate me and I'll be O.K.'. I hadn't allowed for the fact that it was Easter. In the window at the Consulate they'd pinned a notice; 'Closed for three days'. There was nothing else left to do but go to the local hospital where I sold a litre of blood. I was thus able to survive the three days until the Consulate opened. They eventually gave me a train ticket and some spending money. My passport was stamped to the effect that it should be impounded upon arrival in the UK until such time that I'd repaid the money they'd lent me.

"I'd been away over two years, India, the Middle East, Kuwait, Basra, Nepal. During all that time I'd never experienced anything you could refer to as 'culture shock'. But when I got off that train at Victoria, that was the time I felt really weird. It took me quite a time to get used to it. A friend of mine who I'd known since childhood said to me some time later, 'You know, Lari, you were mad when you

came back to England'. It took me such a long time to settle down. I did a bit of this and a bit of that; got an HGV licence, did some lorry driving.

"At this point I met Sue Kelly, Dave's sister. I moved in with her above her mum and dad's place in Streatham. Dave being her brother was just coincidental. My musical tastes were centred on the American West Coast; Quicksilver Messenger Service, Jefferson Airplane, that kind of stuff. I got a job driving with a company called Headley's Humpers. They were a groupage company who specialised in moving antiques and fine art. I'd go of for a couple of weeks with the truck, driving through Holland and Germany, dropping off this valuable stuff at various addresses.

"I was driving this pantechnicon truck and occasionally, if we had a big removal to do, we'd get extra hands in. That's where Dave came in. He was running this band at the time called The Dogs. They played a lot of pub gigs. As I took the truck home with me after work at night, I used to load up the band's equipment, arrive at these pubs and scare the shit out of the landlords. This huge truck arriving.... well. They couldn't handle it! I enjoyed working for the Dogs. They were a good band and I enjoyed what they did. And that, with a basic knowledge of wiring, was how I came into the rock business. I was in at the start of The Blues Band.

"I remember that first gig at The Bridge House taking them all by surprise. I wasn't too involved for the first two months, but once they knew they'd have to become professional, I was taken on, thanks to knowing Dave. It's been 14 years now but I've never planned anything ahead; I take one day at a time. I've worked with quite a few other acts, mostly American bands, but The Blues Band takes up most of my time. There are times, especially in Europe, when it gets me down. There might be a lot of travelling between gigs and over four or five nights you'll get very little sleep. You'll get the gear in the truck and look at the map and think; 'Why am I doing this?' But then we have an easy period and it's all forgotten. Sometimes, after a gig, when the punters have gone and the band have gone backstage for a drink, I often wish I could do that, just leave it. But that's the nature of the job – I have to work then.

"There are times when I've lost my temper with The Blues Band; in fact I've been quite ratty with them on occasions. But they're all of an equal temperament; no one of them is worse than the other. They're professionals and they've been in the business long enough to know what they like. As long as they keep enjoying it, as long as they keep getting the gigs, then if they want me I'll be there."

DAN TOWNSEND

When Nicky's not selling The Blues Band, you are more likely these days to find super-salesman, and all-round entrepreneur Dan 'the man' Townsend man-handling the merchandise. If you think he's related to a Band member – you're right.

NICKY MYAKICHEFF:

Lari met Nicky when she worked behind the bar at the Pied Bull in Streatham, Dave Kelly's local. It used to be said that whilst Nicky was pulling pints, Lari was pulling barmaids. Nicky hails from Cornwall, and the love of her life is horses. She was at one time a noted showjumper, and actually made Wembley one year.

She took over the merchandising from Dan Townsend, Rob Townsend's son, a few years ago, and being constantly on the road with Lari, has become quite proficient in setting up equipment on stage.

T-shirts, programmes, records and tapes are an important adjunct to the complete Blues Band industry. In keeping a business like this solvent and on the road, a band needs the best. With Nicky, they have just that.

Sounding Off

The Front-of-House Views of Des Jabir

Unlike the quiet, thoughtful presence of Lari Myakicheff, moving with smooth deliberation between the amplifiers and guitars on stage, Des Jabir is the animated, wise-cracking alternative sound helmsman of The Blues Band road crew. Des is the man behind the desk at the back of the auditorium. How The Blues Band sound to the audience, and to themselves, is down to him. And if anyone can 'mix it', then Des can....There's nothing tame about Mr. Jabir. He has opinions, some of which could rock a sturdy boat. His relationship with The Blues Band is both fiercely professional yet affectionate. He knows each and every characteristic of the band members; he's impressed and frequently annoyed in the same breath, yet if anything could serve to illustrate some kind of 'family' atmosphere on the road, then perhaps we should see Des Jabir in the role of the clever son who says "Yes – I can mend the TV and the dishwasher, but I'm not making my own bed...." So; what's his story?

Born in London on 7th August 1961, Des's early history seems to contain no indication of his ultimate career. After private schooling, he attended St. Dunstan's College in Catford.

"I left college in 1977. I wasn't particularly good at anything except maths and science, although I did a couple of languages. I'd given up on history and Latin early on, though. My school was a bit of a posh school; we even had an Army & Navy Cadet Corps, and if you didn't attend the Army & Navy periods, you had an alternative which was similar to what you'd now call Community Service. There was a local hospital with a multiple sclerosis centre, and as our community service I'd go along with a couple of the other pupils who played guitars and we'd attempt to entertain the patients, singing folk songs. I didn't actually play, but I went along for a laugh. On the weeks when we weren't required to go, we'd all sit around back at school in the music room, chatting. It was a skive, really. The other kids were in school bands, and I started hanging around with them, setting their amplifiers up. That was my earliest slight connection with music.

"However, although my dad is a doctor and my mother a health visitor, I went on to college to study mechanical engineering. I actually did it for three years, but I quit. I was 21 when I split from engineering. I looked at the engineers I was supposed to aspire to, and disillusionment set in. It was working for a company that spoiled it for me. I could see I

was never going to be able to do what I wanted to. I knew there were ways to circumvent working methods and get things done your own way, but the red tape stopped you. I wanted to think for myself.

"I didn't know what I wanted to do; I thought of joining the Customs & Excise Service, the forces... but I was already a bit too old to do those things. There was no decision like 'I'll make my life in Rock & Roll'; I was messing about on the sidelines with bands but I never gave it any consideration. And an office job held no appeal at all. But if there was a turning point, it was at The White Swan in Deptford. A band called Dumpy's Rusty Nuts, beloved of bikers everywhere, used to play there regularly. That was my local pub, too. Dumpy wanted to organise a coach trip to a pub in Oxford called The Penny Farthing, a popular haunt for him. To get a gig there, he had to take a crowd with him, and as I seemed to know everyone in the pub, he asked me to organise it for him. So that's what I did; began organising these trips. This was at the time when my company, having learned that I'd failed my exams, told me more or less that there wasn't much of a future for me. But Dumpy's band had some gigs lined up with The Blues Band on the Brand Loyalty Tour. He offered me two and a half week's work. I was up for it straight away, because I was also on the dole. I learned a lot with Dumpy, especially in the backline department, and by January 1983 I became self-employed. I was working with a guy called Andy

Keating who was Dumpy's partner in their P.A. company. I learned how to set up rigs and stuff. The day before they did four shows with Supertramp, I set up for the Lyle McGuinness band. Then I worked for the Dave Kelly Band touring Germany. Eventually, after doing some Blues Band gigs at The Mean Fiddler, I joined Will Power, who now work for The Blues Band, supplying P.A. to a variety of acts.

"Call it fate, call it what you like, but since those days The Blues Band have in some way always been a part of my life.

"My girlfriend often comments on what she sees as an inordinate amount of dedication I show them. Maybe she's right, but changes in direction, decisions I've taken, moves I've made, although I wouldn't like to say the band is the dominating factor of my life, they've always been there in the background in some way.

"Do I get tired of touring? Well, some types of touring, definitely. But there's always that one tour, usually the next one, which Dave Kelly will get me to do. I can't get away from it all; it's like a drug. There's always something new and interesting on a Blues Band tour, and if I ever do think I've been over exposed to the Bluesers, then Dave will send me out with Gallagher & Lyle or the Manfreds. My relationship with The Blues Band has always been at a professional level, although there is something else there, that extra draw. Like most human beings, they're all capable of being extremely annoying at times. I mean, I would find it hard to level much criticism at Gary, or for that matter, Rob. Paul, Dave and Tom are capable of being a bit touchy, but I'm talking in the area of the sound here; Dave used to be very particular about monitors in the DKB but he's mellowed on that subject in The Blues Band.

"Over the years The Blues Band have altered. It's much more a 'thinking man's' blues than the old heads-down approach. They've slowed down as they've got older. Sure, they can still do the odd bit of thrash, but they don't do so much of it these days. However, that may only be true of the British gigs, because in Germany, the audience is a much younger one. The German venues often inspire a different kind of performance, much like the early days, than the Civic circuit in the UK. The Dire Straits tour was different again, mainly because all the fans there were Straits fans; it was a mixed audi-ence, many of whom didn't know what to expect. The Dire Straits tour went very, very well. There was a couple of bum nights – Rome and Milan, but the rest were really great. In Spain and France we were very well received.

"The Blues Band has it's characters. Life on the road throws up the odd experience, like Rob at the Redcar Blues Festival, almost not appearing because he'd gone back to the hotel after one too many red wines and gone into a deep sleep. The band almost gigged without him, and I was sent back to the hotel to stir him. Luckily his door was open. But there you go; Rob likes to sit and talk and the longer he does.... well, a fair bit of red wine goes down. Lovely bloke, though; we've had the odd flare-up but it passes in minutes.

"It's the same with DK. Dave Kelly is, these days, the business side of the band. I remember us staying in a hotel in Berlin not long after the Wall came down. Dave comes off stage, in a melancholy mood. He's had a few lagers. We gets into the bar in the hotel and we're ready to continue drinking, but the young guy behind the bar suddenly decided that no more drinks were going to be served to these guests. We weren't misbehaving, or unruly; it was something to do with our credit rating. Dave hit the roof, and insisted that the barman telephoned the hotel's boss at his home to get the bar working again. While this was going on, Kelly pulls out his American Express Gold Card and starts waving it about, in a real 'Loadsamoney' way, saying 'Do you know how much this is worth?!' I'm sitting there with Lari, and once Dave had calmed down, we said 'Do you realise what you were doing just then?'

"But Dave is good at taking on responsibility. He shone on the Manfreds' American tour when things were going wrong. He's developed this commercial persona over the years and he's good at what he does.

"I could tell you about the many occasions Paul or Tom have annoyed me; just fleeting instances. One odd incident I'll always remember, for different reasons, was something which happened to Paul at Leamington Spa Centre. It's quite a modern building. You can drive around a certain part of it, but there are various other awkward parts where you can't. This particular night it was absolutely hissing it down with rain. Paul had missed the soundcheck so we'd set everything up, got the support act's gear sorted and we were about to go to the boozer across the road for a well-earned drink. The door opens and Paul, looking shocked and ashen, dashes in. 'You've got to help me....' he gasps, 'I can't believe what's happened! You've got to come and help me....'

"So, Lari and I put on our jackets and we go outside. One half of the area by the theatre was a paved piece and next to this were some stone steps, descending to where we were. Paul had driven his car right up to the edge of the paved area and over it, and it was now balancing on the sump, teetering on the edge of the steps. Lari got his bottle jack from the van and I got some beer crates. We only had thirty minutes before the show was due to start, and here we were in the pouring rain, jacking the front of Jonesey's car up trying to push it back onto the level area. Lari tells Paul to get in, rev it up and drop the clutch, hopefully getting the car to shoot back in reverse onto the pavement. But Paul blows it.

"In the end, Lari backs the truck up and puts a rope on the back end of Paul's car; with one mighty lurch the car leaps back onto the level ground – whack! I'll always remember Paul's face as he was towed violently backwards across that threshold. He did eventually come up with large drinks all round, but it was a funny sight. As a performer, he can come across to any audience in any language, but if there's a criticism I have of The Blues Band then it has to be Paul's theatricality in performance. He can't help it; that's what he is. The thespian in him will always come out. Of course, you talk to him about it back stage and he'll say 'What? When? I didn't do that....' But in the end you have to face it; the guy can sing and play, and that's the bottom line.

"Tom McGuinness just had to be Irish. He's lucky, and at least he knows it. I remember him saying to me once 'Do you know, I've never really had to work for a living?' And when you assess his career, he's right. He has a knack of being in the right place at the right time. As a player, in the early days I used to find his playing rather irritating, but the years on the road have done wonders. I think it was Dave or Gary who said on the last German tour that Tom was playing now better than he'd ever done, and I have to agree. Out of adversity in the Blues Band have come great ideas; spontaneity throws up the odd surprise. On our recent tour, Paul was rather ill and lost his voice for some gigs. The unexpected is often what

makes good blues. So as an 'unplugged' number, Tom had started doing *Mean Old World*. To fill out the gaps where PJ was missing, he decided to put this into the electric set. He'd do a couple of verses, chorus, then he'd go into a solo; 8-bar, 16-bar, then another 16. You began to get excited, thinking, well, it'll be over soon, so enjoy it, but no; he'd do another 16 and the audience are going potty; and still he'd give them more, and it was interesting stuff, something new in every burst. It just worked, and you could build it and build it; I'd up it and up it in the mix until it was tearing your face off but it didn't matter because it was just.... BIG.

"The Blues Band number both I and Lari hate the most is *29 Ways*; we refer to it as 'Cue the Spontaneity.' We've watched it turn into what it is today. It started off as a perfectly OK Blues Band song, then it gathered all these bits along the way; the theatrical bit, the audience bit, the Bo Diddley bit. It was fine at first but they began doing it in the same sequence every time, hence 'Cue the Spontaneity'. Very annoying. They tried to shelve it on the Fat City tour and replace it with *So Lonely*, but they tried to do the same thing; using that premeditated structure. They started doing it to *Wang Dang Doodle* but they realised they couldn't; it had to develop as a song, in it's own way. Even now it can be pretty boring, but every now and then they hit the groove and get the groove right. But they've now started to approach it from a technical angle; analysing what Pete plays, is Dave riffing at this point.... I just stand there and think Oh...come on guys.... let it happen naturally....

"I thought *Fat City* was a very good album, and I loved mixing it live, especially the big band stuff with the brass and the backing singers. Without doubt they were some of my favourite Blues Band shows. It's a shame they couldn't have worked *Help Me* live; it's one of Gary's best songs. I like everything Gary has written. I've listened to the demo of the album he's never quite finished – where he does duets with Hilary. He really is a very good writer. Sure, he's had his personal ups and downs. He reached rock bottom at one time, but, like most members of The Blues Band, he's had some well-deserved breaks and got to where he wants to be. Take Dave for instance; he's a fairly contented man now. Rob's the same; always fairly happy. No big, grand ideas about themselves. I came across a perfect example of that contentment in music when I worked with Jerry Allison, still the drummer with The Crickets, Buddy Holly's band. I became a good friend of Jerry after touring with him in 1988. I've been to his house in Nashville, stayed on his farm. He's a lovely, lovely bloke. He was over with the Crickets recently – and although this has nothing to do with The Blues Band – it does illustrate the way some people like Rob and Gary stay quite 'ordinary'.

"We were doing a gig – it was Bobby Vee & The Crickets – at the Walthamstow Assembly Rooms. I'd get everything set up for the soundcheck, but they were more interested in finding out where the pub was. So I took them to a decent pub. Jerry is sat there with his beer and this guy comes up, obviously a fan, and says nervously 'Hi.... er.... are you Jerry Allison?' Jerry stands up and shakes the guy's hand, saying 'Yes. Pleased to met you....' Not in a show-biz way or anything like that; just friendly. He sees himself as a guy who farms and makes a few dollars on the side by playing drums. He genuinely believes that's all there is. No 'Legends'; just a bloke in the pub. The fact that he was in one of the most inspirational bands in rock, he shared the stage with Buddy Holly – that's all history. He's a farmer, and that's it, even though we think he's a legend. But there he is, talking about his sheep and his dogs, playing darts. Like Rob, really; Rob can be very self-effacing if you talk about Family. I always think it's a sign of having your feet on the ground.

"How long can The Blues Band carry on? Indefinitely, I suppose. But the problem we have, especially in the UK, is the venues. The old college and university circuit isn't what it used to be, and now we've reached the steady level of doing the civic theatres and arts centres, you can only go around so many times in a year.

"There's always a danger, even if it is accidental, that you'll go back to a place and play exactly the same set you played a year ago. It's not that you've not changed the set; it's just a coincidence that the same numbers will fall together again on that night. I suppose they'll be forced to give it a rest for the odd month here and there just so they don't over-play the circuit.

"But then, you start the year with what looks like a sparse date sheet and then before February's over it starts filling up. They're just a good act and there's always a demand for that somewhere.

"Talking of good acts, I also worked with the Dave Kelly Band in those periods when The Blues Band were out of action. I always thought that, at their peak, with either Mick Rogers or Steve Donnelly on guitar, they were totally unbeatable. It was when Gary, Lou and Mick all decided that they wanted to leave the DKB that we met Pete Filleul. Pete toured with the DKB and we became very friendly, and I suppose it was a natural progression to call him in when The Blues Band toured the *Fat City* album. I really enjoyed the DKB. When they were really cooking, there was nothing to touch them.

"Talking of cooking.... I think I ought to tell you about The Blues Band's eating habits. The Dire Straits tour was something which almost deserves a separate chapter. It was different to the way we usually tour; a very good example of the band living together for an intense period. Take six members of the band, the road crew, and at various times throughout the tour, wives and girlfriends, even kids would come out and join us. Totally unlike the usual European trek.

"Gary had taken his Jaguar on tour. On the stretches when Hilary, his wife, wasn't out there with the boys, Gary used the car rather differently. Something developed called 'The Country Club'. This was Gary, Dave and Pete Filleul. They went everywhere in the Jag, ate at all the best restaurants and had all the gourmet meals, eighty quid bottles of wine, the lot. Paul, meanwhile, had hired a car because Fiona had come out for a while. This left me, Rob, Lari and Tom in the minibus. We were just doing our thing, going from gig to gig. There was full, on-site catering for all crew and performers at every gig. There was a wonderful spread of marvellous food – remember, this is a Dire Straits tour, not the South London pub circuit. Well, the minibus faction, we'd just gather a nice selection of this amazing back-stage grub and put it all into cardboard boxes. On the French and Italian motorways there are these lay-bys with picnic facilities, so we'd become the picnic faction of the entourage. Rob would provide the red wine, somebody would come up with the fresh bread and we'd pull off the road and lay out this huge spread. These were superb feasts. On the days when there were no gigs, we might all end up going out en masse in search of food. Now Dave Kelly, going out to eat, is an experience in itself. He's just heads-down in a mission to find a restaurant; nothing deflects him; he's decided to eat and that's that.

"I remember once (in the UK), we'd done a gig at Malvern. The next one was at Sheffield, so as it was a house PA up there I had time to travel up with Dave and Tom. We were hurtling up the motorway in Dave's car when he suddenly says 'Sunday lunch! We can have Sunday lunch!' So I suggested we took a turning that would take us through Buxton, in Derbyshire. I knew a nice pub there which did good grub. Dave had other ideas. We passed some place and suddenly he hits the brakes, we screeched to a halt and he says 'We'll eat here....' So he's out of the car and across the car park. Tom and I are just getting our coats on to join him when Dave comes scuttling back with the news that there were no tables available. So we're all back into the car. You cannot believe the speed of Dave Kelly when he wants to eat. We're off like a rocket. Fortunately, in Buxton, we had a very nice roast in the pub. Nothing stands in DK's way; it's 'I want to eat – I'm going to eat – and I'm going to eat NOW.'

"Eating on tour doesn't always follow regular times. You might have an odd soundcheck, an interview or an in-store promotion to do. You're not always available when restaurants are serving lunch. But Dave doesn't always see it that way. He'll walk into a place at any odd time and if they've stopped serving he goes berserk. He can be a bloody madman!

"We were in Florence on the Straits tour and we went up the mountain to a nice little place called Fiesole. We all went up; there was Gilly, little Homer (Kelly) was there. But we were too late to eat. Even Dave couldn't alter that. So we had coffee and ice creams. Later, on the way back down the mountain, Dave spotted another restaurant. They were closed but he was pleased to hear that they re-opened at seven. So sure enough, at six-thirty, we were all there on the terrace outside at a long table. Dave then announces 'Actually, I'll not be eating much because I'm not all that hungry....' Well, four courses later he could've fooled me. He managed to do the lot.

"Yes, touring with The Blues Band takes eating to a fine art. The same in Germany. The lads know their way around the menu. Even the talk of vegetarianism, (which gets you nowhere over there) from some quarters of the band, falls apart when it comes around to Schweinhaxe, which is pig's knuckle. We did at one point think of having a European symbol for The Blues Band; it's a red circle with a pig's ankle or knuckle in it crossed with a red bar, like a 'no entry' sign.

"I've been involved with all sorts of bands; country artists, heavy metal. Yet The Blues Band are a constant fixed point I return to. I don't know how long I'll continue this job, it's hard to say. I do have other ideas. But when Dave rings me with another tour, I'm usually up for it. I suppose they keep going because like any other performers of their generation, it's their job, the way they make a living. They've got a few good years yet; just take a look at B. B. King and John Lee Hooker...."

Jersey's pride and joy, The Intruders, with drummer Peter Filleul

Travelling Orchestra

The Peter Filleul Story

Peter Filleul first entered The Blues Band's inner circle through the Dave Kelly Band in 1984. Peter's background differs slightly from the almost text-book rock & roll history of most 60's UK musicians. He was born on 1st May 1951 in the Millbrook Nursing Home, Jersey, in the Channel Islands. His family roots are deep and historical – going back as far as the year 949. The family name was well known for many centuries in the important trade of shipbuilding. This century, however, the family business has been in office equipment. Peter's father took this over from his father, but sold the business five years ago. Mr. Filleul senior is better known on Jersey as a politician where he is a Deputy in the States of Jersey. Now retired, Mr. Filleul senior is regarded as a Statesman; he runs the Jersey Heritage Trust, the award-winning Museum, and is generally a very busy man. Peter's mother died in 1989.

"I attended a minor Public School on Jersey; more of what you might now call a direct grant school. I only boarded for about a year, during some marital impasse my parents were going through. I suppose I did all right, really. Passed 'O' levels across the arts and sciences. It confused the Sixth Form allocation system; if you showed aptitude in Maths and Chemistry you would follow that bias. However, I'd passed maths, chemistry, French and English, technical drawing. So I studied for a year for 'A' level in maths, chemistry and English. I then left school and went to College in the UK to do a HND in Business Studies.

"I'd stumbled into music much earlier, though. When I was nine, I played the drums in a school version of the theme from Z *Cars*. Somebody had to do it; I got the job. I was the only person who could play the drums; I had an Eric Delaney snare drum. In the audience at that recital there was a chap and his brothers who all played different sorts of guitar – i.e., lead, bass and rhythm. We got together, me on drums, and formed a group called The Intruders. We played Ventures and Shadows copies, as everyone did then. We became very successful and made what was, for those days, quite a lot of money. In the end we had all the gear; I had my Trixon drum kit, and the rest of the guys had their Fenders and Vox amplifiers. I was forced to leave the band at the ripe old age of 12 1/2 because my Headmaster wasn't keen on me taking on extended engagements which included not only Saturdays and Sundays but Wednesdays, too. I had my 'O' levels to study for, so reluctantly I left The Intruders behind.

"Of course, it wasn't the end by any means. When I was sitting my 'A' levels, I was playing in a band in the evenings. I would sit in the maths lessons with the drummer compiling lists of our shows whilst doing our quadratic equations. I began to realise that I didn't really want to do maths and English. I had a slight problem in that although I'd had piano lessons until the age of seven, my ears overtook my eyes. I still can't read to play to this day. My music teacher would give me a piece to study; I'd be unaware if the written arangement but because I knew the title I would go away and learn it in my own way. Of course, when I came back and played to him, he'd say 'That's not what's printed on the sheet – if you're not going to learn to read then I can't help you'. It's something I've faced up to at various times; I can follow the score, even to the point where I've conducted orchestras – but sit down and play and read, not yet.

"However, my father said that if I studied for a Business Diploma, and as we had the family office equipment business, then he'd agree to me leaving school. So there was I, 175 miles from the mainland. I had to find digs and be prepared to leave home. I was seventeen. I went to Highbury Technical College in Cosham where I was the only one on my course living in digs. Everyone else lived locally. I had a marvellous time.

"I was doing quite well at college until I contracted glandular fever. It was the time of The Beatles' 'white album'. In common with many young musicians at the time, I thought I could write songs just as good as theirs. My father had already decided that he thought my ambition was to be 'another bloody Beatle'.

"I had discovered that glandular fever is a disease which can also affect your mind. I was back on Jersey. I was the only person on the island who was writing songs at that time. A friend of mine who had stayed out there had become a journalist on the glossy *Islander* newspaper. He decided he would write an article about me. In addition, he said he'd telephone music publishers in London and tell them about this islander who wrote and performed songs locally. The songs I'd written were, incidentally, quite appalling, but I was found appointments on the mainland and one of those turned out to be David Barnes of Essex Music, who then sent me to see John Cooper at Decca Records. He said I should form a band, bring them to London and he would record some demos with me, with the ultimate aim of making an album. Naturally, I was very pleased with all this. Back on Jersey, I went about advertising in the music press and got an English guitar player, an English drummer and a Welsh bass player. We called it The Parlour Band, and after some intensive rehearsing of the material I'd written, I got back in touch with Decca to say 'We're ready!'

"I was dismayed to find, however, that my contact at Decca had left. So I spoke to a chap called Frank Rogers who was then head of A&R at Decca and said 'Look – you've involved me in expense and quite a bit of work, and I have a deal with you....' I was pushing my knowledge of the Law to the limit – 'what are you going to do about it?' He was taken aback by this attitude, but he returned my call and said they would book us into our 'local recording studio'. I said 'What local studio? There isn't one!' The only place capable of recording was Channel Television, so Decca hired the TV recording suite for the periods when the TV people weren't using it. They sent a young guy over, what they called in those days an 'A&R producer'; Nick Tauber, who has since made a name for himself as an independent producer. Nick thought that a weekend in the Channel Islands was a fine thing. He was royally

entertained but on the Monday morning, within minutes of us going into the TV recording studio, he realised that it wasn't suitable, and whatever we did in there was going to be unusable. However, Nick was very positive; he said 'Don't worry about this recording being useless – I'll make sure you get a deal'. And so I did; I got a solo recording deal virtually straight away. I moved with the band to England, The trouble was, the rest of the band thought that that meant they could bring all their material in, and they also brought their friends along. I knew this wasn't going to work; it was a solo deal. Eventually I had to ditch the band. I searched out my earlier musical friends from Jersey. They were all at college up in Leicester. When I told them I had a record deal and asked them if they'd like to go into the studio with me, they jumped at it. And so the first Parlour Band album was made. We recorded in Decca's brand new 16 track studio; we were only the second act in there after The Moody Blues. We rehearsed the album and took the show on tour with Caravan and Steve Hillage's band.

"Things did change in the band, because I realised quickly that I wasn't a lead singer, but our lead guitarist was. He could much better handle all that 'front man' stuff.

"The album seemed to be only selling in tens rather than hundreds, but I do remember one very hungry Christmas getting a statement from Czechoslovakia of all places with a cheque for £165, which made a lot of difference that year. I realised that I must be famous in Czechoslovakia, because I was on a very small royalty and quite a few people must have bought the album for that sum to have been reached. It came to mind years later when I was touring somewhere in the wilds of the mid-west in the U. S. with the Climax Chicago Blues Band. A roadie came back stage and said 'there are some people to see Pete'. Now that usually meant Pete Haycock, who was Climax's star, but on this occasion the punters wanted to see me. I went to the front of the hall and there was this gaggle of young guys saying 'Gee, great to meet you Pete – we've got your album....' and I remember wondering what they were like; there was everyone listening to *Cry of Love* and *Sergeant Pepper* and had seen God, but these kids out in the backwoods listening to the Parlour Band.... well.

"Back to The Parlour Band. Eventually, we

The Parlour Band (Pic: Decca Records)

became disenchanted with Decca. We wanted to do a showcase for all the other record companies so for the purpose of this we changed our name to A Band Called 'O', doing a wider range of material. We were playing a bit of a dangerous game. There was a band called Home who were doing quite well, and their manager, Bill Shepherd, came to see us and liked what we did. We were gigging under both names and attending meetings at Decca where we were saying things like 'oh, we need to be released from our contract.... the band's finished, we're breaking up....' then getting into a taxi and changing our clothes en route to CBS as the new potential signing. And we did sign, as A Band Called 'O', and made two albums for CBS. By this time we were based in Leicester, and I was playing piano. We did a lot of UK and European touring work.

"Universities, clubs, festivals. A Band Called 'O' went on for two years until.... they sacked me. I was fired because they didn't think I had it in me to make another record. This upset our manager at the time, Barry Marshall, because they'd done it behind his back. Within three months of the sacking, Barry had got me an audition with East of Eden, who he also managed. To be honest, I was scared. These people were very accomplished jazz musicians. But I got through and joined them. Our first tour was in Europe, and we had a support act.... A Band Called 'O'. They were surprised but at the same time we all thought it was quite amusing. What must have annoyed them was that here was I, who they'd sacked because they thought I couldn't make another album, in the middle of making one with East of Eden.

"Whilst I was with East of Eden, in the studio where we were recording at night, Barbara Dixon was recording an album during the daytime. She had just finished a run of *John, Paul, George, Ringo & Bert* at The Lyric Theatre in London. She was looking to change her drummer and one of her guitarists in favour of a new drummer and a keyboard player. It was all extra work and I put in for the audition. She came down to the studio one night to check if we were well behaved gentlemen or not, and soon after I learnt all the stuff on the tape she gave me. After attending the audition with the drummer, Jeff Allen, we got the gig. However, this turned out to be more than a gig in the end. I became very friendly with Barbara which resulted in me being sacked from the band. I was out of work for nearly six months.

"I saw this advert one day in *Melody Maker*, 'English band with American hits about to tour U. S. require keyboard player'. This sounded intriguing. I answered it. A couple of days later I got a phone call; it was The Climax Blues Band's manager inviting me to an audition at Air Studios. I'd toured with East of Eden as support to Climax and I felt comfortable with the idea, but when I got there there was a huge queue of keyboard players. Once again, I prepared carefully by learning all their material, so that when I went in to the audition I could play all their songs and fit in fairly well. The fact that they already knew I was a reasonable sort of bloke to tour with certainly helped, and I got the gig. I rehearsed for two days with them at a sound stage in Shepperton and then we flew out to America, where *Couldn't Get it Right* was number three in the charts. I was completely in a daze; they were a big, big band.

"I arrived in America and was met at the airport by a limousine which took me to the Ramada Hotel. In my room there is a bottle of brandy, bunches of flowers and the champagne flows freely. Suddenly, more than ever before, I feel like a 'pop' star. From being on the dole I'd played with this band for two days and now this complete luxury. That was the beginning of 4 1/2 years with Climax. I recorded two albums with them, toured extensively, especially in America. I enjoyed working with them, although Climax have a very American attitude to what constitutes 'blues' music.

"They were due to make another album in America but as I wasn't signed to the American record company I wasn't allowed to play on it. However, they still retained me to play on the tour promoting this new album when they came back. I had to wait about eighteen months for this album to be completed. Unfortunately, at the end of this wait, they called me to a meeting to inform me that they were, in fact, going to get another keyboard player. Even more unfortunately, though, they told me this before they'd asked the other player to join. As things turned out, the new guy turned them down as he wasn't keen on the terms they offered, and you guessed it; I got the job of playing the European tour, me, the man they'd just sacked. A further responsibility developed on that tour because their manager, Tony Brinsley, had to go home when his father died. As I was deemed to be the most well behaved or reliable character in the band, I ended up with the additional post of tour manager, collecting all the money for the band which had just fired me.

"One of the most pleasant memories from that time with Climax was recording the very first album at Air Montserrat. It was during the great 'Winter of Discontent'. We flew out to this paradise on January 2nd and completed the album by April 4th. Three months in heaven on full pay. That was really something, utter bliss. I also appreciated whilst I was there my non-contractual connection to the band, because they were spending, or should I say, 'investing', hundreds of thousands of pounds of their own money whilst I was just there on pay to play, having a good time. Whatever the album was costing wasn't really my concern.

"Climax were good for me; they showed me the world, introduced me to the big tour, and it was a well spent 4½ years. The added bonus was that they introduced me to me good friends, The Blues Band. I first met them on a German tour.

"By the late seventies Climax were playing back in the UK and it was about this time that I first came into contact with The Blues Band. There is an element of confusion in the histories here. Climax insist that they had it in their contract at several UK gigs that they would be supported by The Blues Band. But The Blues Band insist that they had it in their contract that Climax were supporting them. To add to the confusion, Chris Runciman, who became The Blues Band's front-of-house sound man, was at that time sound man for Climax. It was all wheels within wheels.

"Back in London I was introduced to the playwright, Willy Russell. I had written a song with Willy, *Dance The Night Away*, and this had been recorded by Climax. The song, incidentally, was a ridiculous Bee Gees pastiche with sax solo on the key changes. It was number one.... in Pennsylvania. Willy and I became musically close and he asked me to go up to Liverpool and help him on a musical. I spent a year in Liverpool working with Willy on what opened on the 6th January 1983 as *Blood Brothers*. My work with Willy introduced me to television. After *Brothers* opened he was asked to provide a title song for a Central Television series called *Connie*. I worked on that with him, and I was then asked to provide the incidental music, which was adapting and amending themes that were hidden within Willy's tune.

"*Blood Brothers* moved down to London, where I was trying to develop my music publishing company. I published Willy's music and my own, plus a few other bits and pieces. I was making demos, sending them out to people who were making records – about 150 went out. Dave Kelly got one of my cassettes and liked a song called *Come Back to Me*, which Willy had written and I'd arranged. Dave recorded this on his *Mind in a Glass* album. I played some synthesiser on that track. He then asked if I'd like to tour with the Dave Kelly Band. In that band line-up we had a problem guitarist; his problem was drink, and this led to acute unreliability. We were in Italy when the leader of the Communist Party fell into a coma the night we were due to play in Milan. The gig was cancelled and this gave us the perfect excuse to fly home and have one quick day's rehearsal with the wonderful guitarist, Ed Deane. We ditched the drunk and took on the extraordinary Ed instead – a very good move.

"Roy Battersby of the BBC had approached Dave, asking him if he'd provide soundtrack music to *King of The Ghetto*. Dave knew I'd had experience with soundtrack work and asked if I'd help out. We really enjoyed doing that soundtrack and it introduced Dave to a lot of people. We did all the pre-production in my studio. Dave is a very intuitive player and he ought to be doing much more of that kind of work. I co-produced with Dave his *Heart of The City* album, and after more TV work, I was asked to do the soundtrack for *Life and Loves of a She Devil*, which got me a BAFTA nomination. I did more work for the same producer, David Henshaw; the *Marksman* series with Roger Daltrey, on which I worked with Richard Thompson, and *Jumping the Queue*. This led on to the documentary series about living on low wages and the dole, *Hard Cash*. It was supposed to be put out by the BBC but they chickened out. They had already been accused of political bias by the government on three previous items, and *Hard Cash* would have been the fourth. Legal problems were also responsible for its shelving. The whole series was pulled and has never been seen. The accompanying album is a work we are all proud of. It was done on a very low budget, brilliantly organised and all recorded in five days.

"At the same time I was working with Richard Thompson; a witty, accessible and charming man, spontaneous and wonderful to work with. We worked on a Hollywood Film called *Sweet Talker* which was never released in the UK. It was produced by Taylor Hackford and starred Bryan Brown. Doing the Hollywood movie was great; Richard was great on that soundtrack; we enjoyed California, running around on the MGM lot.... great.

"I then did another BBC series for David Henshaw called *Global Detective* (which was also shelved) and a thing for BBC Manchester called *The Racing Game* – a six parter about horse racing, about which I knew little at the time. There's been a wide variety of work.

"Today I'm busy developing my music publishing and consultancy business. We've handled the affairs of various composers, some from the National Film and Television School. We handle the music for Philip Appleby's *Rarg*, which has been a great success. We've done another cartoon, called *Balloon*, the music for which was composed by Julio D'Escrivan. Producers, composers; we help them with everything we can. Contracts, for instance. It is interesting and rewarding work.

"And, of course, since Jo Ann Kelly's death I've been working on pulling together her tribute album. I'm stuck at the moment at a certain point, but I know if I can get Eric Clapton on board and Johnny Winter, then people like Bonnie Rait will follow. They all had a special place in their heart for Jo Ann. I'm sure the album is going to happen; it's just a question of when.

"I first came to record with The Blues Band on the *Back for More* album, and the year after was asked back to work on the *Fat City* sessions. I must say that I like the way The Blues Band work in the studio; they seem to do their arranging at the mix. Everyone comes along to sessions with different ideas about what to do, and then at the mix stage, they'll bring this in, keep that down, it's a kind of democratic process until they reach a sound they all seem happy with. Of course, this spirit of co-operation can sometimes dilute a track's potential, but that's the way they work and I like it.

"Of course, I'm not really a regular, full-time member of The Blues Band. I've been brought in when and where required, for the 'showcase' gigs, for instance, when *Fat City* was launched, and especially when they toured that album – with my keyboards I could duplicate all that brass and orchestral backing – 'textures' are what I supply, and I'll keep on doing it on and off until they sack me!

"I know that Bob Hall would like to be doing more gigs with the band but now that he lives up north that's not always possible. What Bob does I could never do; he's steeped in the blues piano style and although my background is pop I'm far more of a 'general' player. And there is the question of economics to consider. If a gig seems right, and both Bob and I can make it, then that's great. But often the band have to make a choice; it all depends – do they play two keyboard operators or one? They always sound great, anyway – pianos or not!

Peter Filleul 1990's style at home in his studio

Serious left-hander – Gary Fletcher

Stetsons, Blues and Racing Cars

The Gary Fletcher Story

Gary Fletcher was born 'within the sound of Bow Bells' at St. Thomas's Hospital down by the Thames on 25th October 1951. The Band used to call him 'the baby'; at 42 he's finally lost the tag. Gary's initiation into the busy world of British R&B was in many ways quite different to that of his Blues Band colleagues. Unlike many musicians there's an atmosphere of the sportsman about him; he moves in different circles with his interests in Formula One car racing, and almost achieves the impossible between gigs by having a full time job as UK managing director of a successful Scandinavian company. Whatever Gary Fletcher does, he does well, and music has been a dominant factor during three decades in which, like Dave Kelly, he's seen his fortunes ebb and flow. Today, there's more flow than ebb. Songwriter (*Green Stuff*, etc.), record producer, left-hand bass player extraordinaire, captain of commerce, ladies and gentlemen.... Gary Fletcher.

"My dad was a policeman. He came from Liverpool. We grew up in the bottom half of a terrace house in South London. There was me and my sister, who's eighteen months younger. We used to spend quite a lot of time, on holiday, Christmas, Easter, up in Liverpool; Widnes, actually. My mother was Welsh. She met my dad during the war. He was a bobby then but he went into the Navy. I suppose you could have called us working-class, economically, but with some middle-class pretensions. I went to grammar school after passing the Eleven Plus. I was a bad schoolkid in some ways. I blotted my copy-book really early on. I got mixed up with a bad crew. Not really bad in as much as we went around nicking stuff; there was none of that, but we caused a bit of bother and tended to be rebellious; long hair, scruffs, that kind of thing. We bunked off a lot too. I was quite good at football and cricket, that sort of stuff, but I failed all my 'O' levels. Sport kind of kept me alive. I did eventually get an 'O' level, in metalwork. I'd re-sat my 'O' levels in the fifth year. Steve Gurl, my mate, was there too. I'd met Steve when I was ten and he was eleven, and we've been mates since. He went out with my wife, Hilary, before I did.

"Steve and I had a mutual interest, slot-racing. It was a glorified form of Scalextric. We got very clever at it and we entered the national championships as a team – and we won. We were the national Schoolboy Team Champions in 1966 and we sud-denly got a lot of respect at school. Although we were in the same school year I was at the start of the year and he was at the end so I won the senior championship and Steve won the junior.

"We got hired by an American company who made slot-car parts and so we left school and straight into our first job. We used to tour for these people, demonstrate; it was great. Then Steve packed it up, I kept going for a while until music came along. We discovered music together. Steve had had piano lessons and had a piano at home. Now, this puts me in context alongside the other members of The Blues Band. The first blues album I ever heard was by Eddie Boyd. But it wasn't an Eddie Boyd Chicago album – it was Eddie Boyd with Fleetwood Mac. We realised that this was pretty good stuff; it was simple. I got a bass and started to learn the bass parts, Steve learned the piano parts. Being left-handed, and not knowing how to swap the strings around, I had to learn to play a conventionally strung guitar but upside-down, which is the way I still play. I never had any other aspirations to be anything other than a bass player. This was the period 1969-70. I got into a band very quickly, even though I could hardly play at all. My sister was going out with somebody in a band – he was the drummer. The band's bass player was good to look at and he had the gear, but he couldn't play much either, so because I knew the bass lines to *Spoonful*, I was in. The band was called Breath of Life – a three piece of what I would call 'limited ability'. However, we did win a talent competition in Brixton Town Hall and from that we got offered a contract to play in Italy. It actually meant going to live over there, but my old man wouldn't sign the papers to let me go. In those days you had to be 21 to do these things, not 18 as it is today. As a result of this I had to leave the band. They got someone else in and went to Italy. I was choked at first until a few months later they came back absolutely penniless after being totally ripped off. In the meantime, Steve and I put this little band together and we played in a pub in Streatham, The Crown & Sceptre.

"The landlord of the Crown & Sceptre was Alan Cornick. His stepson was Glenn Cornick, who played bass with Jethro Tull. Glenn left Jethro Tull and he'd left all his amplification equipment stacked up on the stage in the pub. So me and Steve approached Alan and asked him if we could use it, and do a Friday night spot in the Crown & Sceptre. So we formed a great little band. There was no drummer, just bass, two acoustic guitars, Steve on piano and two girl singers. We were called Garfield Road. One of the guitar players was John Blackmore.

"Glenn turned up and formed Wild Turkey, nicked John, then took Steve as a roadie. By the time Steve was 19, he was touring the States with Glenn. John got fed up of the touring, left, then Steve took over as Glenn's keyboard player. It was Glenn Cornick who loaned me the best first decent guitar I had. When I started I had a Hofner Fender copy, which cost me twenty five quid. Glenn lent me an EB3, which to my delight was the same bass that Jack Bruce used. He was my idol and the reason I started playing. I'd heard Cream's *Wheels of Fire* and I really thought it was the business. Anyway, it was a couple of years before Glenn got his bass back. He lives in L. A. these days; I think he's an accountant with a food company. He was a nice bass player, very melodic, but I don't think he was up to being a band leader, although Wild Turkey did make two or three decent albums.

"Through Garfield Road I met quite a few people. I wanted desperately to be a pro musician at any price. One of our girl singers left and went into the business world. She's on the board of Laura Ashley now. For me though, it had to be music. In those days you could get a job easily; it wasn't so much

looking for work, it was 'what can I do to avoid it!' I had the answer. I went to college for a couple of years, ostensibly to catch up on my lost education, but really it was a good way of skiving. In vacations I did a variety of jobs; stacking parts in a motor factory, driving a furniture van. I was living in a house in Norbury with some mates. It was the classic student house-share scenario – absolutely great. I was the youngest.

"There were lots of ladies – no trouble in that department. I was playing in one of the best bands I've been with at the time. There was a jazz club in Thornton Heath run by a bloke called Vic – Dave knew it as well. Alan Elsdon used to play in there on Monday nights. I was in there one Monday and we heard that Alan had got a residency at Ronnie Scott's and was leaving. Vic came up to us and said 'You lads play a bit – fancy coming along to do the odd gig?' There wasn't going to be any money in it, but he said he'd put the hat round for us. Paul Holden was playing sax with us. He'd been with various soul bands and he was quite an influential guy – he showed me the ins and outs of experimentation and he just broadened my horizons. He led me into differnt music, introduced me to people like Terry Riley. Paul had a mate who was a great guitarist.

"So it was sax, bass and guitar. No drums again. I was depping in a soul band at the time – the Front Line Band. Anyway, we turned up at the jazz club with this trio for the first gig and there were about ten people in the audience. We had a bass amp, a guitar amp and a little p.a. system. Paul had this little transistor radio with a lead attached to it. He would walk up to the P.A., put the radio on top of the speakers, flick the dial and wherever it landed, that was the tune. He didn't tell us what we were supposed to be doing; he just started blowing and we followed him. I think we got about two quid each. Well, we went back the next week and there were forty people there. So we'd obviously created a bit of a buzz. All the free-form jazz nutters were turning up; 'Oh, yeah, baby! Like.... get down, maan!' I was in a totally different area of music.

"I met this drummer called Tony Maloney. He'd been taught at Trinity College and knew his stuff; in fact he teaches drums today and one of his pupils is Sam Kelly, Dave's son. Tony invited me to join a band called Gnasher. It was just after Curved Air; the band had two violin players, both from pretty

Innocent, Young and Hairy: '70's Fletcher

well-heeled backgrounds. Anyway, they put this ad in the quality press – *The Times* and *The Telegraph*; 'Progressive Rock Group based at the Royal Academy of Music seeks financial backing'. I mean, these guys had dads like bishops and stuff like that. Believe it or not, we auditioned to financial backers in the Mozart Room at the Royal Academy. It was all pretty impressive. We had some pretty serious enquiries. In the end we settled for this Taiwanese businessman who didn't seem to want to put too much pressure on us and he slipped us ten grand!

"We went out and bought this monstrous P.A. system, a mixer desk, a synthesiser. We didn't play 'songs'; we played 'pieces'. Hardly any singing – I had to introduce that. We had opus numbers; it was all very pretentious, lots of wiggly-wiggly arty farty stuff. I mean, we could turn *20th Century Schizoid Man* into an afternoon drive! It was weird. We did university gigs but in the end it all ended up like East of Eden because these two violin players, although they were classically trained, they could

knock out a good jig between them and we ended up rocking. But we went down really big. Gnasher did record but it was never released. It turned out that the Taiwanese bloke only saw us as a tax loss and really he didn't want us to earn anything. He paid our wages, though, and I got a Hi Watt amp which I use to this day in The Blues Band.

"Meanwhile the free jazz thing continued and we had the club absolutely jammed. We got a drummer who was with a fine band called Major Surgery – they had Don Weller, and we even had people like Henry Lowther on trumpet turning up. We were still flicking the old dial on the tranny and improvising; it got out of hand. People were coming up to us after gigs and waxing lyrical; 'Oh, the beautiful harmonic structures and the esoteric expressionism and interplay....' We knew it was all a load of bollocks, and the minute it started involving all these other people it began to be pre-meditated; the spontaneity was killed off. We were simply too stoned and pissed to know what we were doing – mind you, I

Writers, producers and long-time friends: Gary with partner Steve Gurl

think most of the punters were as well, but there were all these musicians getting up to blow; Mike Westbrook, people like that; I didn't know who the hell most of them were, all I knew was that they lived in the area. It was weird. We just stopped doing it; I think it was because I got a properly paid gig, I'd seen an ad in the back of the *Melody Maker*: 'Folk rock band require bass player'. I thought, that's me.

"Garfield Road used a lot of my material and although it wasn't exactly Fairport Convention, it did have that early acoustic folk feel to it. I was quite a melodic bass player in those days; you'd never know it these days. So I got the job but it wasn't what I expected. It was Bryan Chalker's band. At the time he was the only UK country singer with a major record deal. It was guitar, fiddle, mandolin, claw-hammer banjo. Adrian Legg was the guitar player – what you'd call a 'seminal' guitar player in Britain

now. So off I went and did the country & western circuit for two years. And I did really well out of it. Steve Gurl was on a £25 per week retainer with a record company which was good money in '73–74; but I was on a steady hundred notes a week. To be fair to Bryan, we didn't exactly do the regular country stuff like *Okie from Muskogee*; we got near with Johnny Cash's *Ring of Fire* but we did a lot of Shel Silverstein material and, believe it or not, we had a hit record. We recorded *Help Me Make It Through the Night* before Gladys Knight got it. We were with Decca's Chapter One label, produced by Les Reed, and we got to the dizzy heights of number forty in the charts. It was good. We made a good living.

"Bryan Chalker went on to become a journalist and Adrian Legg went on to become an even better guitar player. I got into a band which rehearsed and gigged like mad – Panama Scandal. This was two years, '75–77. We had Jimmy Knox on drums, Jon

Blackmore guitar and vocals; he's a photographer now. Fraser McIntosh played keyboards and left to go into publishing, Nicky Wood, the guitarist, quit the business altogether. We worked hard with Panama Scandal, but Punk came along and the scene altered completely.

"I came to what you'd call 'real' blues late. When I first heard Muddy Waters it hit me like a sledge-hammer, and Howlin' Wolf, although not to the same extent. My idea of blues, apart from that Eddie Boyd album on Blue Horizon had been Cream, Hendrix, stuff like that.

"But by now I was catching on fast and filling in all the gaps in my record collection; B. B. King, that kind of material. With Jimmy Knox from Panama Scandal we formed Sam Apple Pie and played blues right through '77–78 until we just ran out of steam. Steve Gurl, my old mate, had been with Babe Ruth and we got back together again as a songwriting duo. We wrote a lot and were looking for a publishing deal when we got a record deal with Logo. We had a single out which didn't do too badly, then in mid-78 I joined Dave Kelly in The Wild Cats. This came about just by accident. I was earning a crust by mini-cab driving and one day this bloke asked me to take him to Heathrow on a 'wait & return'. I'd been sat around waiting for a fare and this was a Godsend; virtually half a day's work.

"We got talking and he turned out to be Wilgar Campbell, Rory Gallagher's drummer. Eventually he mentioned this band and through that I met Dave Kelly. Dave and I got on well and when I found out about The Blues Band's first rehearsal, somehow or other I managed to get in. You know the rest.

"At one time, in the earlier part of The Blues Band's success, I was utterly into the whole music biz thing. Production, writing. I was heading towards record production. I had to build up my part in The Blues Band over the years; I kind of sneaked in through the side-door, so to speak; I had a different background to Paul, Tom and Hughie. Hughie was a good influence, too; he introduced me to various things. And being involved in the writing; yes, I am proud of writing *Green Stuff* but it's only a small part of what I'd like to do.

"Today, although I really enjoy being in the band, I have to say I've had a re-think about the business itself. There's a whole lot of back-stabbing and nastiness which you don't get in ordinary commerce; I mean, take my day job. It's straightforward; we run a salesforce, sell a good product and tackle the competition. It's clear-cut and you know where you are. To be honest, I like the commercial world and I'm at home in it. But some of the creeps and politics I had to deal with in music; you could be perfectly open, naive and honest, but the minute you showed signs that your talent might be getting you somewhere, they'd smile at you to your face while they were stitching you up behind your back. Yes, I'm older, a bit wiser, and enjoying other ventures. I'm getting into car racing, enjoying my kids. Hilary, my wife, is making a career out of writing. The Blues Band is a nice thing to be in, and I'm lucky. I've said it before, but I've survived so far with a very limited bass technique and a lot of chat. And the band? How long will it go on? Don't ask me. That's anybody's guess!"

Lou's crew – The Dance Band

"Might as well be me . . . ."

The Lou Stonebridge Story

"Can I just say how important Lou Stonebridge was in the development of The Blues Band, especially in the early years. Lou and I produced the first two albums, but because I was in the line-up it was Lou who had to do all the work in the control box. I remember doing *I Go Crazy* – the James Brown song and, incidentally, the first song the band ever performed – and we wanted a song like that and we had the beginnings of *Come on In*. Paul, Lou and I worked on it – actually in Paul's theatre dressing room – And Lou wrote *Find Yourself Another Fool* and *Hey Hey Little Girl*, *Hard Working Man* and *Might As Well Be Me*.... He was a very important factor in the band"

Tom McGuinness

Lou Stonebridge was born in Bury, Lancashire on the 21st June 1948. The first evidence of his musicality occurred at a very early age on the top deck of a bus coming home from Bury market when he burst into an impromptu rendition of Mario Lanza's hit, *Be My Love*.

"My mum's brother was a real Elvis fanatic. He used to do the complete Elvis soundalike thing. In those days you'd have a piano in the pub and people would get up; he'd always do the Elvis songs. He had all the American 78s: Buddy Holly, all that stuff. In fact the only British act I liked at the time was Lonnie Donegan; he was a great influence. Next came stuff on TV, like *Oh Boy*, and then the big breakthrough when my dad bought a portable radio. Up until then we had two hours of 'needle time' on the BBC Light programme and maybe David Jacobs on Saturday night (if you were allowed to stay up that late!). Then of course there was *Saturday Club* with Brian Matthews and that was about it. But it was Radio Luxembourg which got me listening – with my mate Steven Priestley – to American music. We were eleven. Friday nights became record nights. He had all these U. S. 45s, exciting stuff like Sandford Clark. Eventually my parents bought me my own record player. I remember the first three records I bought at six shillings and eightpence each – exactly a quid's worth; *Pépé* by Duane Eddy, *You're Sixteen* by Johnny Burnette, and *Are You Lonesome Tonight* by Elvis.

"But I discovered this second-hand record stall on Bury Market. I was suddenly hearing stuff on the Chess label and Tamla. It was hearing Jimmy Smith playing organ on *Walk on the Wild Side* on Jack Jackson's Luxembourg show which convinced me that I would ultimately play the organ. My grandad still had an upright piano and he lived around the corner. The first tune I learned to play on the piano was the solo from Nat King Cole's *Let There Be Love*. At about quarter to eleven one Tuesday night I was illicitly listening to Luxembourg under the covers when I heard Marvin Gaye's *Can I Get a Witness*. It was never played again but it had a great effect on me. That was the first black pop record which made me realise there was something else out there.

"Steve and I eventually progressed from just listening to music to actually playing. Steve had an acoustic guitar and I had a Hofner with a pickup and a Watkins Westminster amplifier. Trouble was, he was tone deaf. To this day I can't read and write music; I can roughly follow the dots, but with Steven I had to learn the chords, count the bars and he'd tap his foot and count when to change. This went on until our first gig – I was fourteen – it was Valentine's Day, 1963, at the Gladstone Liberal Club in Bury. My grandad was the social secretary there and a band had let him down, so we had a chance. On the three gigs we played there, we had a different name each time. The first one was as The Strollers. I remember there was only one microphone so for the instrumentals Steve had to mike his guitar up and play acoustic for the vocals. We also used the house drummer. The drum kit was like something you'd see in Bob Kerr's Whoopee Band; a strange sight with the huge bass drum. The drummer used beaters instead of sticks, with those round pom-pom heads. I remember we did a version of Jet Harris & Tony Meehan's *Diamonds*, and when we reached the bit where we expected the drum solo, I turned to the drummer and yelled 'take it!', at which point the head flew off one of his beaters into the audience. We also had a music stand which I had all the chord sheets stacked on; I remember that falling over more than once and things got really confusing.

"This all lasted about six months until we became The Everglades. My dad worked with a guy who was a bass player with a band called the Dominators. They were a level above me; they had all the gear and did working men's clubs. They had pink Fender Strats and Selmer Selectatones and the bass player had a Hofner Club 40 bass. It was a real business. I was fifteen and they were all seventeen and eighteen – at that time they all seemed to be so much older. Plus the fact they were all working and I was still at school. But I got an audition as their singer and landed the job. It became Ian Curtis and The Dominators; we did Cliff and the Shadows stuff, as everyone seemed to at the time.

"Eventually I began to realise that all the good stuff was on Chess and mostly written by Willie Dixon. The first British R&B record I bought was *Country Line Special* by Cyril Davies; that immediately inspired me to take up harmonica playing. The band were still into The Shadows because they came from the Rossendale Valley and there seemed to be a time warp there; I was trying to interest them in Chuck Berry records and they'd try and play *Johnny B. Goode* still with all the echo and I'd be saying 'No.... no! You don't need that!' Although I was young I was very determined and formed an alliance with the rhythm guitarist and in time we managed to change the whole set in favour of Chuck Berry. I was still Ian Curtis and they were still the Dominators. But I thought that the change in music warranted a change in name so we became.... Curt's Creatures.

"At this point my dad had some influence again. We sacked the band's manager, who was the guitarist's dad. He was a watch repairer and also involved with pigeons. We used to get a lot of pigeon fanciers in our crowds, and I used to groan and think: 'How the hell will *Country Line Special* or *Chicago Calling* go down with this lot?' We got around to

making a record. It was a demo and we cut it at Harker & Howarth's little music shop studio in Bolton. It was a four track EP which had on it *Get on The Right Track Baby*, *Chicago Calling*, *Country Line Special* and a track by me which I can't remember. It was my first recording and I was sixteen. Anyway, as I said dad helped us in firing the manager and he took over in the job and did quite well. We got plenty of work.

"I remember doing my 'O' levels – I suppose the general plan was that I was going to be a quantity surveyor or something. I suppose that, despite the music, my parents thought I would go back to school and do the 'A' levels. But even at 'O' level stage I was not allowed to go to school. My headmaster asked me 'Is the length of your hair absolutely necessary for your evening occupation?' I replied that it was. 'In that case'. he said, 'as you finish your school life in five weeks, when you come in to do your 'O' levels you'll enter by the back door and leave by the back door. I don't want you in school in the meantime....'

"Still, I got five 'O' levels. I got a job with Co-operative Insurance in Manchester. On the band front, however, something happened which was quite unexpected. We'd done an audition for an agency and on the way back we stopped at a chip shop. It was my turn to get out of the van and get the last pie. It was Russian Roulette; a car hit me in the street and I was hospitalised for six months. Things fell apart for the band after that, but the agency were still interested in me so they put me together as singer with this band called The Raging Storms. They'd played in Germany and they were into Soul, Motown and Blues.

"It was a good time to be going out to gigs, too. I recall one night going into Manchester and Stevie Wonder was on at The Oasis, Lee Dorsey at the Twisted Wheel and Wayne Fontana was in town, too. I'd already seen Rod Stewart at an all-nighter in Manchester. We used to play a lot of supports at Rawtenstall Astoria. I remember supporting the Sir Douglas Quintet when they had *She's About a Mover* in the charts. It was all good experience.

"The Raging Storms were all full time professionals but I was still working at CIS. They would pick me up outside the office and we'd zoom off to Newcastle or somewhere and I'd get back at say, five in the morning, get washed and changed and be back at work. It was a hard life, although we were young....

The 'progressive' era dawned. I was listening to John Peel. We'd done a test recording for some-one.... I can't remember who.... anyway, it was *One Fine Day*, the Chiffon's song, and it was a disaster. We did a week in Torquay at a ballroom. The we got a London gig at the Playboy Club on Sunday nights as a try-out. Previous to this we'd done our first 'London' gig in what I fondly thought was London at that time – Romford. The promoter was a.... well.... tough character from the East End, but he did put us up at the Madison Hotel in Sussex Gardens. This, as far as I was concerned, was rock 'n' roll; the Madison, where there was always eight or nine transit vans parked outside. London was for me. We were committed. The band was going through drummers and bass players, but we did this audition for the Playboy Club and we passed. All the arrangements and ideas were worked out by me on the keyboard, and I then showed them to our keyboard player. But I was just so frustrated, because I knew I wanted to play that

organ. It came to a head. My mother cashed an endowment policy, I got a new organ, stayed home for a week and rehearsed like mad. When the week was up, unfortunate though it was, our keyboard player had to be told that he was no longer with the band. Once again I decided the bass player wasn't right. We got a new guitarist, too. We changed direction and the name changed to Glass Menagerie.

"While we were at the Playboy, we were introduced to the producer, John Schroeder, and we got a test with him. He then put us in touch with two managers; Maurice King, who at that time handled The Walker Brothers, and Mike Rispoli, who worked for the Gunnell Agency. At the time I was managing the band myself. The band at this stage was doing a cross between blues and 'west coast' stuff; Jefferson Airplane... we even did *Light My Fire*: a real mixture. Also, I was now writing material. I was 20 years old and I recall after a Saturday night gig at the Playboy, when we had to go back up north the following day, having to attend two meetings that Sunday morning before we left. One was with

Peter Hope-Evans and Lou in full flight

Maurice King and the other was with Mike Rispoli, and I had to decide who would manage us. I remember being at home that night, lying in bed trying to decide. I knew that the Maurice King option would mean the big TV shows and more money, but the Gunnell thing was where our heart was. So, we chose the Rispoli option and landed a test with Pye. This was the time when Status Quo were recording *Pictures of Matchstick Men*, produced by John Schroeder and we then recorded three singles for Pye. The first was the Stones song, *She's a Rainbow*, the second was *You Didn't Have to Be So Nice* done in the style of Vanilla Fudge, and the third was a Harry Nillson song *I Said Goodbye to Me*. We wrote the 'B' sides. The first two were done on four track and we did the third on what was then an experimental eight track at Pye in Cumberland Place. Radio followed. We were doing David Symonds, John Peel, David Hamilton. It all went very well.

"Eventually, Chas Chandler became involved with the Gunnell Agency and Chas became our manager and producer. We recorded a wonderful album which unfortunately never saw the light of day. I've tried to track down the master tape, as we've since wanted to put the album out, but even Chas doesn't know where it is. During our time with Chas we had a couple of good singles; *Do My Thing Myself* and quite a cut 'b' side *Watching the World Pass By*, then a ballad, *Have You Forgotten Who You Are*.

"It fell apart. We went out as a three-piece; our guitarist had suffered a nervous breakdown. We were organ, bass and drums. Then we got a call one night; 'Pack your bags; you start a tour of Germany tomorrow....' and off we went, supporting John Mayall. It was good, but our swansong.

"I went back up north to put another band together. We had a good following up there. I'd heard this band called Grisby Dyke. I took them over basically, and we rehearsed with the idea of becoming something like Glass Menagerie 3. However, I got a telegram from a man I'd met down at the Speakeasy. He said I should telephone this number in Gloucestershire. I phoned and this guy said 'We need an instrumentalist and singer to join this band we're putting together called Paladin....' The two guys were the organist and drummer who had been with Terry Reid. I got the job, singing and on this occasion, playing piano. Unfortunately Grisby

Dyke/Glass Menagerie never got off the ground. I also took the guitarist with us and the roadie.

"We did two albums, and a great plus at the time – Roger Dean drew the covers, which are now collector's items. And I've learned recently how popular we were because at the moment I'm writing with John Edwards, Status Quo's bassist, and he says he went to see Paladin six times – they were one of his favourite bands!

"Eventually, that too faded. They cut back and replaced me and the guitarist with a guitarist/singer. They began touring without an album and faded away.

"I began working solo; guitar and amp, 40-minute slots up north in working men's clubs. I was travelling up north every weekend. One day I got a message from Geoff, our old Paladin roadie. He was working for Manfred Mann at the time. He said that Tom McGuinness was putting McGuinness Flint back together and was looking for a singer who could play. I turned up at the audition at New Cross with the *Guardian* under my arm, which half-got me the job, but after playing Jerry Lee Lewis's *Crazy Arms* things fell together. I got the job.

"When McGuinness Flint finally folded, Tom and I, as we were now writing songs together, were put on a retainer by our publishers. It basically meant that for about the next three years we just wrote from Monday to Friday, keeping our hand in with the odd gig here and there. This period will no doubt dovetail in with Tom's story.

"We met Rob Townsend one night on the train when Tom and I were on the way to my place to do some writing. There was this guy called 'Bob the Taxi', who runs a blues thing at the Turk's Head, Rob's local, in Twickenham. Bob had this little blues/skiffle outfit. He didn't need drums – his feet were loud enough.

"Together with Rob, Steve Mullins on bass and eventually Tom McGuinness, we did this Monday night spot. We began doing things then as 'Rudy & The Rialtos' and we had a Christmas single out called *Christmas Tears Will Fall*. It's a great single and it has Wolfman Jack on it; we recorded it, sent it over to Canada, and he put his voice on and sent it back. That was on Gull Records. We got a deal with Air Records and cut an album, using their new computerised suite. In the other studio, if I remember rightly, Gallagher & Lyle were doing their

Breakaway album. I recall us playing the Albany in Deptford – Rudy & The Rialtos charity gig – the warm-up support was Dire Straits. I can just about remember them doing *Sweet Nothings* and maybe a couple of Ry Cooder songs. I remember thinking 'Hey.... they're good....'

"I became involved with production. Incidentally, prior to The Blues Band period we produced some tracks for Paul Jones. These were *Sweet Rock & Roll* and *Sweet Talking*, both of which were written by me and Tom, and *I Want to Be Happy for The Rest of Your Life*. I remember the engineer on those sessions was Murray Latham who went on to work with Ian Dury and Paul Young. Then we got into Cool King Records. Our writing contract (Tom and I) with Heath Levy, was drawing to a close, and Ray Williams, who as you know managed The Blues Band for a while, got Tom and I a deal with RCA. We did an album – even had a small hit – *OOee Baby* – it made the 50s. But when our publishing contract finished, we decided to form a company of our own. We were recording and publishing Gary Fletcher and Steve Gurl amongst others; The first record was *Stax of Tracks* by The Dance Band. In theory it should all have been a wonderful thing. Now, with hindsight, I realised it was one of the

worst things I could have done. It became 'a business'. One of the biggest disappointments, mainly due to poor distribution, was Dave Kelly's single, *Return to Sender* missing it's chance. Perfect record, from a great album, four or five plays on Radio One every day and we couldn't get it in the shops. That one hit could've changed Cool King for the better. We got so enmeshed business-wise towards the end. It was liquidated. Relationships became soured.

I felt Tom and I were a good team. Tom has the most incredible memory, so you can never win an argument with him. Tom's forté is his ability to put people together. He recognises the right people – take The Blues Band as an example. Even to this day, someone can call Tom up about some person or other and he'll have their phone number to hand and he'll bring those people together. People say he's 'incredibly lucky'. I don't believe that; it's just that he can always see an angle, he stores information, has this memory.... that's what he's good at.

"Tom telephoned me one night and told me that they were putting a blues band together. He asked me if I was interested. I thought about it, but imagined it was going to be a very heavy, serious thing. Do I regret not joining? Well, once I went on to discover the kind of band it was and the material they were doing, I thought yes, that would've been right up my street. On the other hand, I doubt if I could have lasted all those Blues Band committee meetings and the internal political wranglings of the band.

"I will say this: I did my first gig as a solo support act for The Blues Band at the Beck Theatre, about July '92. Dave and Gilly, Gary and Hilary; they're all what I like to call close friends, and Rob and I go back a long way. Take into account also my relationship with Tom. Yet there seemed to be no feedback or response. I was just any support act. In fact, it took me five or six gigs before I got any response. It demonstrated to me that, as a unit, they are very exclusive and cliquish. There's not much warmth comes from them if you're anything of an outsider. I did talk to Gary about it, but he brushed it aside with 'Well.... you know what we're like....' But bearing in mind my involvement over the years I find it very

odd. And I don't mind you including this; I've done my 'tour of duty', so to speak.

"The Dave Kelly Band was a different thing. It was a such a good band but there was a lot of barbed comments made about the way it finished. It finished really because me, Gary and Steve Donelly knew we simply couldn't afford to keep on going. On the other hand, Dave is a good band leader, and we didn't want to jeopordise Dave's album, and we wanted to see it through. I don't know if Dave Kelly knows it, but the track on that album, *I Believe in You*, was actually written about Dave. It also incorporated other band members' *'People won't say a word until they've had a drink....'* and the chorus; *'When the chips are down, and there's nothing left to do, and it all comes round – I still believe in you....'* That was all for Dave.

"Today I'm still writing and performing. I'm currently working on material for Status Quo which may or may not be successful. I've had some disappointments; I would've liked to have been in the 'first division' of rock; the premier league. But today I'm doing exactly what I did when I started. I'm playing and writing for sheer fun, with the added bonus of being paid for it. The best sensation you can have is writing a song and then one day hearing it being played on the radio. That is *the* medium. Unfulfilled ambition? To have a hit record.

"I like my day job. I've studied wine, and I'm now qualified to the level of one grade below Master of Wine. I love being in the studio, and I love opening the show for The Blues Band. I feel a major sense of achievement doing that; going out solo like that is really laying your head on the block. Any applause you get in that situation is undiluted; as there's no-one else on the stage, you know it's all for you. But I now accept that music is always going to be second to the day job, unless of course that I write that number one single or album track.

"All things considered, I'm lucky. If I can go out there, play what I play to an audience who are prepared to listen, then what more can I ask?"

"The Best Since Otis Spann"

The Bob Hall Story

Jazz Life Journal said of this man "Bob Hall has worked with the best simply because he is one of the best". Not seen as often as The Blues Band fans would like to see him, Bob is none the less one of the very cornerstones of the world of European rhythm and blues. Since moving up to Sheffield in recent years from his native London, Bob is not as available for gigs as he once was – and surprisingly, for a player of such immense talent, he has never abandoned his day-job for a full-time career. As a busy patents lawyer, he finds his full time career almost as fulfilling as his music. Founder member of The Groundhogs, Savoy Brown and Rocket '88, Bob, like his long-time partner Dave Kelly, has played with them all; Chuck Berry, John Lee Hooker, Little Walter, Fred McDowell, Alexis Korner, Charlie Watts and Jack Bruce to name a few; and he is featured on over 85 albums. He started playing at the age of 11.

"It was the early '50s when I first heard Winifred Atwell playing boogie woogie. Real blues? I first heard that from a schoolfriend. Apart from collecting Nazi memorabilia, he collected blues records. A 10-inch Clarence Lofton, a Hooker 45 and a Howlin' Wolf EP on London American. Wolf did it for me; *Smokestack Lightning* is still one of my all-time favourite records. I took piano lessons from Mr. Heckman, a German gentleman living in Brighton. He'd played with Stephane Grapelli, and when Grapelli's life was featured on TV, on came Mr. Heckman, my piano teacher, as one of the guests.

"My father was a great piano player. At home in Bermondsey we had a lot of parties. I recall how popular he was and I thought 'yes; I'd like to be as popular as that....'

"It was hard, just having my boogie woogie, to fit in anywhere at first. In the 1950s, the skiffle groups were around, but they didn't have pianos. But when I heard Humphrey Lyttleton's recording of *Bad Penny Blues* (which I do these days with The Blues Band), things began to look up. I was still at school and on Wednesday afternoons I would play truant. In my bedroom I had this big old radio and on Wednesdays at 3.45 on some European station a French jazz critic called Hughes Panassie hosted a blues show. I would sit by the radio, scribbling the lyrics down. I also listened to Jack Jackson on Radio Luxembourg. He often played releases on the Specialty, London American and Imperial labels. Not many, mind, but enough to keep you listening. If I could keep awake that long, at 11.15 the *Voice of America* came on and played stuff like the Newport Jazz Festival. It was on that station I heard the whole of Muddy Water's Newport set. Potent stuff!

"I went to Durham University to read for my degree. I came down to London as often as I could. Chris Barber was at the Marquee in Wardour Street. He'd been in Chicago with his band in '58, and the result was that you could go and watch his first set, all the trad jazz stuff, and in the second set on would come Alexis Korner and Cyril Davies performing blues. This was a very tempting period for me – having to keep going back to Durham – but I stuck at it and finally got my degree. By this time I'd seen Sonny Boy Williamson gigging with The Yardbirds, more Cyril Davies, lots of blues, and I knew what I wanted. I answered an ad in the *Melody Maker* for a piano player and landed an audition with a band called The Dollar Bills. I wasn't all that good, but I got the job. The guitar player with the band was Tony McPhee. Before long we changed our name to The Groundhogs and I found myself up on stage backing John Lee Hooker on his first UK tour. He had two singles in the charts – *Dimples* and *Boom Boom*, and suddenly, dreams seemed to be coming true.

"We went on to back other artists; Jimmy Reed, Little Walter and others, but it was Hooker who actually taught us how to play the blues. This opened the door to lots of gigs and tours over the years. I played with Chuck Berry, Howlin' Wolf, Muddy Waters, Mississippi Fred McDowell, Bobby Parker. They all had something to give, and they were all memorable for different reasons. Take Chuck Berry, for instance. A lot is made of the man's legendary awkwardness, but I found him fine. He dropped you in at the deep end; he'd tell you nothing – no keys, anything; he just started playing and you'd have to follow on and learn. And that's what we did; we learned very quickly. But I had no problem with Chuck.

"Old Fred McDowell was a nice man but it was a bit awkward playing with him. He was much better as a solo performer, yet he just wanted to be a front man of a band. We'd often tell him, when he tried to get people up on stage with him, 'Do it on your own, Fred.... you're better on your own....' but you couldn't convince him. Little Walter would have us in hotel lobbies sitting at his feet, showing us how this or that blues number should be played. And Howlin' Wolf? I can't find enough superlatives to describe Wolf. A true and total gentleman, whilst at the same time, a strict disciplinarian. He could be very forceful if you didn't get it right, but he was fair. John Lee Hooker, on the other hand, if he wound up with a bad backing band, would just turn up the volume on his amplifier and forget they were there.

"I sat in with Muddy Waters at the Marquee when he was playing a double-header with Bobby Parker. I was playing for Parker – naturally Muddy didn't need me – he had Otis Spann! But that particular night I learned all about showmanship and quick thinking. Muddy was fit in those days. He had a routine where he would lay down on the stage to play whilst Otis Spann left the piano and danced around. This night I took over on piano. It was earlier that same night, though, and I was at the keyboard playing in the key which Bobby Parker played everything in – C sharp. Anyone who plays the piano knows what a swine of a key that is. I knew Otis would put in an appearance during our set, and sure enough, he came out on stage to great applause. Parker turned to Otis and I vacated the piano. 'Take it, Otis!' shouts Parker; and I can remember the look on his face when he realised the number was in C sharp – a totally awkward key. I thought, rather cleverly, 'Well, Otis Spann, that's got you!' But no way.

"'Take it, Otis!' was immediately followed by Otis leaping up onto the piano stool and playing the piano with his feet, to tumultuous applause. Showmanship, bravado, call it what you will it's what sets the great aside from the ordinary.

"My latest CD, *At the Window*, is really my first proper solo work. It's been well-received and I'm proud of it. But some of the line-ups I've recorded with are really memorable. After eighty albums you sometimes tend to forget just how many good players are out there. My work with Dave and Jo Ann Kelly on the *Tramp* album, released in '69, is something I'm proud of. We also had Mick Fleetwood in the line-up. I did quite a bit of the writing on that, too. It was a good band and a good album; our single got plenty of airplay but the label, Spark, wasn't up to it. You can still get that album – it's on CD now on See For Miles records.

"And there was a great piano album I made with the late Rolling Stones pianist, Ian Stewart, and another piano player, George Green – *Jamming the Boogie* on Black Lion. To add icing to the cake, I had Charlie Watts on drums. A very nice album and well received. It was pointed out by the critic Francis Smith that it was the 50th anniversary of the release of the very first boogie woogie record, so to commemorate this Alexis Korner and I, after a discussion at a Professor Longhair concert, decided to expand and augment a big band I was involved with, Rocket 88, by bringing in Alexis, Charlie Watts and Jack Bruce. The whole thing was held together by Ian Stewart. We were to make a record to mark the 50th anniversary of boogie woogie. We already had trumpet, trombone, two tenor saxes. With a line-up like that the fans would queue around the block. I was amazed at the dedicated attitude of band members and the trouble they'd go to to get to a gig. Alexis would jet in from somewhere; we'd be playing in Holland and Charlie Watts would be gigging in Paris with the Stones, come off stage and drive all the way to Holland just to be with us. It was a really nice period.

"This was followed by two years lay-off for me, due to illness, during which poor Alexis passed away.

"Although I enjoy playing in a band situation, and especially with The Blues Band, I am after all these years beginning to see myself as more of a solo artist. Back in those early days it was simply the blues; I had no time for out and out rock. I think British

Left: the late Alexis Korner (left) with Bob Hall at the piano in the 1970s and, above, in 1994

artists did actually create a whole new tradition in the blues; we used to feel self-conscious and apologetic about the way English or British blues bands sounded – their difference from American bands, for example – but these days it is that British sound which has its own peculiar quality. We don't need to apologise anymore. The cross-fertilisation the Brits created put the blues back in the limelight and illustrated to many young Americans in the sixties just what a wonderful heritage they had, hidden, right beneath their noses. I was at a festival recently in Lugano and an American bass player came up to me backstage and said 'Are you the same Bob Hall who played with Savoy Brown?' I told him I was that man, and he replied 'You guys got me into the blues – you started me playing....' And although some critics wouldn't like to admit it, the likes of Eric Clapton really can have an effect on a new black blues album. Take that great singer, Marcia Ball. When she began her career in the U.S., she was listening to British blues albums. She said to me recently "I can't remember who recorded it but there was one particular record I played a lot, called *Make Me A Pallet On The Floor*.

"Actually, that recording was by Jo Ann Kelly. You

listen to Marcia Ball today – there are echoes of Jo Ann still. So don't let anyone underestimate the influence of British blues.

"I never gave up my day job for one good reason; I like it. I remember when Savoy Brown were offered the big U.S. tour and they issued an ultimatum; come with us or leave the band. I stayed at home, but told them 'You're only playing the blues – you'll not make any money....' But they did, of course. I have no regrets. I've played with the best and I continue to learn and still love what I do. My own personal accolade, what I regard as a small acknowledgement of whatever I've achieved, can be summed up in this little story. Mike Rowe, the blues writer, was in Detroit doing some research on the great 1940s player, Big Maceo. He went from bar to bar, asking what the scene was like back in the 1940s. In one bar, he asked an old black piano player, 'Is there anyone left these days in Detroit who plays like Big Maceo?' All the other old guys shook their heads, but the pianist said; 'Aint nobody around plays like Big Maceo; 'bout the only guy I know who plays like him is a guy in London called Bob Hall....'

"Now that really made me feel as if I'd achieved something...."

Blues Brother – Soul Sister

Jo Ann Kelly

Who was Jo Ann Kelly, and why is she in this book? If you're a newcomer to the Blues, or well under fifty, or even just a dewy-eyed Paul Jones fan, then this is a question you're no doubt asking. For a start, she was Dave's big sister. That's reason enough; on odd occasions, she might stand in with The Blues Band; she's on the *Live* album. But mainly, Jo Ann Kelly was the essence of British blues enthusiasm. If Dave Kelly's voice and guitar smell of Mississippi, then Jo Ann was Mississippi. A lady of no compromise, what she heard in those early years – Memphis Minnie, Bessie Smith, Fred McDowell – that was what she wanted to do, and no one on the British scene came even close to her achievements. Canned Heat wanted her, CBS thought they had her, and at the Memphis Blues Festival, Johnny Winter wanted her. But she side-stepped fame and fortune; not deliberately, but simply through a judicious avoidance of hype. Thus, she remained closer to her music, if sadly distant from the better income she thoroughly deserved, until her untimely death in 1990. All you need to know about Jo Ann Kelly can be heard on her wonderful album *Retrospect* on Document's *The Connoisseur Collection* (CSAP LP or CD101) from 44 Seymour Place, London W1H 5WQ. So important was her contribution to the world of Blues that a full obituary appeared in all the main UK papers: *The Times, The Guardian, The Telegraph* and *The Independent*. Sadly missed is an understatement. On the afore-mentioned album, Paul Jones writes this in his sleeve notes:

"May I leave the last word to Bonnie Raitt? 'It was hard to do *Walking Blues*, for instance, but I was not born with a voice like Mavis Staples or Jo Ann Kelly....'"

If there is a Heaven, and Jo's in the choir, then dying doesn't seem too bad a prospect after all. The following piece *Fish, Chips & Legends*, was first published in The Blues Band Newsletter, *Ready* in the winter of 1990. I had thought of writing something new on Jo Ann for this book, but the swell of emotion at her death produced this article and although it isn't an obituary in the traditional sense, it is a very personal interpretation of the effect she had on those who became her friends.

You remember certain days for certain reasons.

I recall, for instance, June 1st 1974. Wendy and I were visiting friends, Alan and Margaret Curtis, on a remote, windy farm at Sunk Island on the bight formed by the north bank of the Humber. We were all incredibly poverty stricken, hoping that life would turn soon for the good and filling in the waiting months and years with a frenzy of home-brewing, child-rearing and listening to old blues albums. It was a bad time for music. The sixties had evaporated into a mess of wide lapels and velvet flares and we would comfort ourselves on wet afternoons and balmy nights with our scratchy vinyl memories, wondering what became of Chicken Shack, John Mayall, et al, lubricating the starkness of finally having to 'grow up' with Boots Best Bitter, baked potatoes and Bukka White.

Indeed, it had rained that afternoon, and as we sought some fresh air on a promenade around the cow-sheds, I remember picking up Alan and Margaret's tiny daughter so that she could speak to a nearby inquisitive Hereford. Our son, Martin, slept peacefully in his pram, and his sister Sarah sought knowledge from a cowpat with a damp twig. I knew the answer, but I couldn't help asking Alan the question.

"Why did you name your daughter Jo Ann?"

"After the greatest white blues singer who ever lived", came Alan's reply, in his lovely, rolling Beccles accent.

At about four in the afternoon we went back to the tiny tied cottage, cranked up the record player and through Alan's enormous speakers listened to the plush tones of the Lady herself, an experience which can perk up jaded eardrums just as hot wholemeal toast can cheer a bitter winter breakfast.

At 4.53pm a huge explosion rocked the whole estuary; only four or five miles away the Nypro Plant at

Flixborough exploded, killing 28 people and damaging nearly 2000 factories and shops.

I felt that explosion again at 10am on the morning of 23rd October 1990, when Gilly Tarrant telephoned us with the news that Jo Ann was dead.

As the proverb goes, fate leads the willing but drives the stubborn; through it (but more through The Blues Band) I finally got to meet Jo Ann Kelly one cold November Saturday in 1981. It wasn't in the glitzy afterglow of some brilliant gig but in the cosy domestic ordinariness of Jo and Pete's little house in Acacia Avenue, Mitcham. I was already overawed to be in the company of Dave Kelly, who I was interviewing for *Guitar Magazine*. We'd gone over to Jo's to pick up a guitar and I was tingling with a fan's excitement at the prospect of this added bonus. She emerged from the kitchen, tea towel in hand; not the gritty Blues Goddess of a flabby northern hippie's imaginings, but a bright, shining and plain woman. If you'd looked into Jo Ann Kelly's smile and felt the lean strength of her genuine handshake you knew immediately that you'd made a friend. And believe me, Legend or not, that's what Jo Ann became.

Perhaps it was something to do with years spent in the sharkpit called 'The Music Biz', but like her brother, Dave, Jo was equipped with a finely tuned bullshit detector. I like to think the needle didn't flicker too much that November afternoon as I burbled nervously about my friends who'd named their daughter after her. That night we went to a party at Tom McGuinness's house and on the train home the next day I felt like a pilgrim returning from Rome. For the next week I did nothing but brag and drop that Lady's name.

During the months and years which followed I was invited into Jo and Pete's house on many occasions. When most travelling salesmen were tucked up in some Belgravia fleapit with a can of Carlsberg and a black and white TV, this one spent nights most blues fans would have fantasised over; in the pub with Dave or chewing over the gristle of life in the eighties at Acacia Avenue. There was always a bed and a meal in a Kelly household, no matter how late I arrived.

In the early eighties, before I succumbed to the fact that I was not, after all, a potential concert promoter, I was daring enough to promote mini Kelly 'tours' on Humberside. We even crammed the whole DK band into the Submarine Bar in Cleethorpes, but with a draw like Dave or Jo Ann even a financial disaster like yours truly could make a few bob. June 1983 remains one of the happiest summer memories for Wendy and I. It was gorgeous weather and I remember how proud we were to have the trusty Kellymobile parked on our driveway. I'd always promised Jo the true splendour of real fish &

chips and the four of us took the afternoon air outside the Cleethorpes Pier Hotel. A couple of pints of Tetley's was followed by a visit to Ernie Beckett's Fish Cafe in the Market Place. I can see Jo's eyes now as she marvelled at the size of Beckett's Jumbo haddock. We left Ernie's place stuffed with fish, chips, bread, butter and tea, and many times after that Jo would say "We must go back for some more fish...."

Jo gave generously of her time. Her wealth didn't come in the end from signing big record deals, touring with Canned Heat or being moulded into a sequinned shell by the 'product people'. Far from it. Jo Ann Kelly liked to feel her feet firmly on the ground, she liked to look around her and feel the same comfort she'd always felt from familiar spirits – the spirits of her home, her friends and the unassailable purity of her music. She could be receiving a standing ovation one summer night and the next, (as she once did) meet Wendy, Sue Breese and Mary Kelly for a night of open-air Shakespeare. This was her wealth, and she shared it with us all.

There was an overflow of caring goodness in Jo's life; when Ellie came into the world there was a lot of love stored up for her. Here were the perfect parents, and now, the loveliest child. Reading Ellie stories, making her laugh, always reminded me of talking to Jo Ann. Like her Mum, Ellie has that sparkle, a questing innocence, a dash of impish mischief. Pete has a real legacy from his happy years with Jo. At least Ellie will help to slowly fill some of the sad void her mother's death has left.

The last time I met Jo Ann Kelly was one warm summer morning at her new house in Park Avenue, Mitcham. Pete was out somewhere and Jo had been on the telephone most of the morning doing what she found so time-consuming; getting gigs. She had dismissed her operation; she was bright, positive yet stoical about the unpredictability of her ailment. She felt good about her career. I made Ellie laugh, we drank tea and Jo said "This year I'm going to make it...." Later that day, driving home, I thought about her earnest smile and wondered just what 'making it' meant. To us on the outside, the untalented, the gaping audience, the term remains a puzzle. Perhaps in the end only the artist knows when they've 'arrived'. For us, Jo Ann Kelly 'made it' the minute she strapped on a guitar and pushed that mellow, autumn voice into our eager ears.

As part of this tribute I make no apologies when I admit to writing the following review in *Folk Roots* magazine in June, 1986. I saw very little of the gig in question, but I sure as hell heard it. As for the 'patient roadie' in the corridor, I'll let you figure out who that was.

JO ANN KELLY,
Baysgarth Theatre, Barton-on-Humber.

The ice still clings to the south bank of the river, huge slabs of stubborn, grubby snow streak the quiet feet of the Humber Bridge. Christ, it's cold.

About a hundred of the curious have pierced the black bitterness and sought out this petite legend, wondering the same as many; how does she sound now? Was it that, back in (painful cliché imminent) 'the sixties' our native bluesers sounded good because they were here and Mississippi wasn't?

Early Jo Ann Kelly recordings are a thing of rare power, bearing all the rip-raw drive of a freshly-fuelled chainsaw. Well, none of it has left the lady. What tonight's show demonstrated was just how much more control, variety and entertainment this three-piece line-up offers. From Bessie Smith classics like *Me and My Gin* a whole host of Memphis Minnie gems through to a spine-tingling rendition of Billie Holiday's *You've Changed*, Ms. Kelly enveloped us in a warmth and fondness for her material which made this night something special. The trio is perfect and balanced for this showcase of adult music; John Deacon is adept at that particular brand of boogie 'n' barrelhouse piano most of these period pieces demand, and to complement the lady's own strident acoustic, Pete Emery's battery of electric guitar styles accentuates and drives home every song with great subtlety.

In the darkened corridor outside the auditorium an incredibly patient roadie paced up and down nursing Ms Kelly's tiny daughter, Ellie. I hope she grows up to sing. What a team she'll make with Mum. Maybe Mississippi is here, after all.

Somewhere on Humberside a young woman called Jo Ann Curtis will look at her father's record collection and see a singer with a name like hers. If ever she walks past Ernie Beckett's Fish cafe, and looks at the table near the window, I hope she realises that a Legend once sat there.

Streatham to Memphis, Cologne to Cleethorpes. It was a long haul, Jo, and we're still applauding.

"But if the while I think on thee, dear friend,
All losses are restored and sorrows end."

Shakespeare, Sonnets 23

JO ANN KELLY, Blues Singer;
Born Streatham, South London,
January 5th 1944, Died October 21st 1990

Time-served blueser, Mark Brooklyn, meets a friend at the Cambridge Folk Festival in 1992

Pat Stirling accepts a welcome, but confused, visitor to Scotland on the Fat City Tour

Fans

Followers of The Blues Band devoted enough to need a regular flow of information on their idols are a diverse group in many ways. In 1980 the accent was more on 'bluesology'; the band's source material. John Mayall was in Laurel Canyon, Eric was lost in his Armani suits. But here at least were some original pioneers of British blues, on our local stage, in touch and still telling it the way it ought to be. Audiences then were students, bikers, heavy metallurgists with a respect for the genre's roots, and long-time Paul Jones fans. Fifteen years on, in the UK, this has changed somewhat; a much more 'respectable' audience, used to theatre seats and rarely prone to bopping in the aisles. In Europe, of course, and especially Germany, the spirit of '79 still lives. Venues on German tours still accommodate that original 'sweat on the walls', heads-down thrust of old. There are festivals, special events, and massive flights into the stratosphere, like the Dire Straits tour.

And at every gig, a newcomer, a changed life. They write in for information and the 'family' has a new member.

There are fans, fanatics, obsessives, seekers of information too embarrassed to be 'fans'; loud fans, quiet fans, and – superfans.

Superfans of The Blues Band tend in general to be female. There was always an unofficial crown for these 'queens' and they come from all age groups. The first 'superfans' were Diane Hutchinson, who worked regularly at The Half Moon in Putney, and Annette Blusch, from Germany. Male fans of the early period tend to burn intensely for a year or two, then vanish into married, mortgaged manhood. The women are more faithful. Take Diane, for instance; although now married and living in Scandinavia with a family, she wouldn't dream of missing her newsletter or a new album. Annette Blusch is now a successful record company executive, but remains a firm 'blueser'. There are levels beyond this mild devotion, however. Here's the 1990's superfan – Surrey's one and only Danie Winwood-Jones, writing for her University newspaper.

The first time I saw The Blues Band was at Glastonbury in 1988. I'd heard Paul on the radio, and already knew of Tom and a little about the R&B bands of the '60s. I just had a feeling on this stiflingly hot June night that my taste in music was about to change for life.

In the Acoustic tent that evening, I was jammed tight by the growing crowd against the stage. The atmosphere was electric; you could have set light to a fair-sized field with it. The moment I saw Paul for the first time, I realised why. He looked so young; surely this couldn't be the man the programme said had been around the blues scene for over 25 years? I was captivated by this cheekily grinning, brown haired man, his head through the curtains, sticking his thumb up at the crowd. The curtains were whisked back and the band played searingly fast blues. Before I had time to take in the great musicianship, Paul was waving and smiling as he launched into I just Wanna Make Love to You.

"By the time he's finished, I thought, I'll be wanting him to...."

After a dozen songs at a blistering pace, the house lights went up. Paul was on his knees and singing to a girl nearby. She responded, and so we had an audience participation number, 29 Ways. Such noise you haven't heard since those films of Beatles concerts. I joined in, wondering if my heart would hold out if he came any closer to me. I wasn't lucky that time (four years later in Guildford was my turn to share his microphone) and a good thing, too, as by that time, I was shocked to discover my voice and I were parting company.

All the way through the set, Paul kept up a barrage of witty comments and sinuous movements. I still don't see how he has the energy, but I love his stage technique to pieces. I stumbled away from the tent somewhere about midnight vowing to go and see him again as soon as I could....

Besides Paul's voice and steaming harmonica (as an instrument of pleasure) the live viewer needs to beware Dave's lethal solos, Tom's green strat, Gary's rock-solid bass and Rob's Ginger Baker-esque drum solos. Don't say you haven't been warned.

Since that first night, I've seen all their South of England gigs, and Paul singing Cole Porter twice. Each album is a 'must'.

I can't analyse what it is that makes The Blues Band so alluring. Paul's magnetic personality combined with excellent musicianship, with little need for synthesised sounds. They have a true feeling for what they play; they are moved, the audience is moved. Down to the River and Work Song at the Guildford festival broke my heart so audibly I was sure the band could hear it.

Thanks for the first 15 years, guys; keep going and here's to the next 15....

DANIE WINWOOD-JONES

Male perspectives are not so readily available, but here's one from Cologne:

You British often fail to know how lucky you are. The Blues Band are part of that foundation of English rock and pop which transformed original American R&B into something else, more accessible in our European culture. The great thing about the generation The Blues Band are from is that although they transformed the music, they kept the central emotion of the Blues intact. It is great to know that these great originators and interpreters of classic material are still enjoying what they do, still paying respect to the giants of the genre like Wolf, Hooker and Muddy Waters, whilst at the same time having as much if not more fun than men less than half their age. The Blues Band are a joy to us in Germany. I only hope the people of the UK know what a national treasure they have in Dave Kelly, Paul Jones, Tom McGuinness, Rob Townsend and Gary Fletcher. Long may they reign!

GUNTER KRAUZE

And fans worldwide like to tell you what's happened at particular gigs. From Worthing, in Sussex, for instance:

At the end of July, Ted (my other half) and I were at the Gosport festival. Naturally, we were there to see The Blues Band. During the early part of the show Paul seemed to be having trouble with his radio mike. He asked us if we could hear anything, and we all listened as a little voice came out of the speakers, clear as a bell: "Gosport Security, Gosport Security".

When the laughter died down Paul told us this true story. He was appearing some years ago on stage in a production of Pilgrim's Progress, playing the part of Christian. Christian is agonising about what he should do and he turns to another character called Evangelist,

and pleads: "What should I do? Tell me, what should I do?" Just then, right on cue, loud and clear and echoing around the theatre, a voice from a nearby radio-taxi service said "Go to 129 Laburnum Gardens!"

Paul's mike was quickly swapped for a different type and the Gosport show continued, minus interruptions from Gosport Security....

ANNIE HOOD

Fans keep the whole show going. Take for instance those keen hawkeyes who keep track of any media mentions of The Blues Band; professional cuttings experts who scour the press – Kim Laydon of Newcastle-upon-Tyne, Pat Ali of Bradford. Really good photographers like Richard Austin, with his better half, Linda, of Brighton. Pictorial archivists who travel hundreds of miles in a day – Pat Stirling and family of Glenrothes up in Fife, Scotland. Here's Pat's testament:

I first saw The Blues Band in March 1981 in Dundee when they were featured in Radio One's In Concert. I knew very little about them and had sent for the tickets as a surprise for someone else. I knew I would enjoy seeing my 60's pin-up, Paul Jones, but I was quite unprepared to become totally hooked on another band member – Dave Kelly. The highlight of that gig was Someday Baby and to this day this is still my favourite.

After that gig I lived and breathed Blues Band, videotaping their TV show, A Little Night Music, playing this and the albums constantly. They became an obsession. My seven year old son Neil became a fan and knew all the songs off by heart. At Christmas his grandad toured the Edinburgh music shops to find him a harmonica identical to Paul's. Neil wanted to go to the next concert and in September 1982 he got his wish. He spent a week making a playdoh model of P. J. complete with a cotton bud microphone. I tried to explain that we wouldn't actually be able to talk to the band but he was determined he would take his model along anyway.

When we arrived at The Playhouse I gave the parcel to one of the doormen and thought no more about it. During the interval one of The Blues Band's road crew asked if Neil would like to meet the band after the show. It was hard to concentrate for the rest of the concert. In the dressing room Neil took it all in his stride, chatting away to everyone whilst I just went to pieces. I was so nervous I knocked Gary's pint over. Everyone was so friendly and it was a great chance for me to ask Dave about his solo work. Everyone was so friendly; Dave took my address and promised to keep in touch with dates for the Dave Kelly Band. We left on cloud nine....

Although it was a year before another concert, it was worth waiting for. I received a postcard from Dave Kelly himself, inviting me to see the Dave Kelly Band at St. Andrew's University and I was on the Guest List! I went to the gig with my two brothers and their friend, and whilst we were waiting, Dave came out of a side door and he actually recognised me. Backstage we were invited to the Edinburgh University gig the following night. One funny point that evening was when Dave made a comment about someone calling them a 'Mickey Mouse' band – unaware that I was in fact just about to present him with a 'Minnie Mouse' for luck. (He hadn't seen the Minnie Mouse at this point) so we were all in stitches over that. The next night in Edinburgh was great, too.

Over the next year my personal life was in a terrible mess. I had to bring up my two sons on my own, and life was quite a strain. We saw The Blues Band, (my sister and I) at The Edinburgh Playhouse, met Dave in the bar, chatted like old friends. But I didn't know at that point that it would be five years before I saw them again.

In 1987 I married David and became Mrs. Stirling. He knew about my Blues Band/Dave Kelly following, but seemed more interested in Depeche Mode, The Cure and Japan, etc.; but things were to change. First of all the October 1989 Back For More edition of the newsletter, Ready arrived. Having never been to Aberdeen before, we found ourselves in the car park of Caesar's Palace and who did we bump into – yep. Dave Kelly. He insisted we were on the Guest List. I introduced David and was amazed when the concert started because he joined in everything with great enthusiasm. We were back on the trail. The next day we were at the Glasgow performance and met Bob Hall and John Fiddler, had a great time taking pictures and chatting.

During the coming months we went to all their Edinburgh gigs – three in a row. My boss, Anne, was with me and finally got to meet her hero, Paul, who gave her an impromptu rendition of Summertime *backstage. On the last night we took Neil and Colin. Neil had been seven when he last saw the band – now he was fifteen. At the concert they were 'Jones'd'; they had to sing the chorus to* 29 Ways. *But the best was yet to come. During the harmonica break on* Blue Collar *Paul played* Summertime. *It was so lovely; I was in tears, and at the end of the song he bowed in my direction. What a night. The band afterwards went out of their way to make us feel welcome.*

After Glasgow in May 1991 we had a long wait of four months; we were invited to the Town & Country Club in London for the launch of the Fat City album. The great day arrived and we set off, first for Eastbourne(!) on Thursday morning, arriving at my cousin's after a twelve hour drive. Next morning we had a quick tour of the town, lunch, then off to find the

Town & Country in Kentish Town. Our trusty Metro took us to Finchley, where we had our first experience of the tube. At the venue we soon met up with Dave and Gilly, as well as Lari. It was a night to remember. Rob Townsend called us 'silly buggers' for travelling so far 'just to see them....' Then we met the famous Roy and Wendy and the camera went non-stop. Unfortunately we couldn't stay as we were driving all the way back to Glenrothes. It was a long journey back; we slept in a lorry park at one point – but it was a weekend to remember for a long time.

At subsequent gigs we took Colin and Neil – Colin now a dedicated 'Uncle Jack' fan and pleased to have his book signed. Neil had his picture taken with Paul, standing back to back – such a difference from the September '82 pic!

I had been off work suffering from depression and it was good to relax. We went to the next three concerts, and then we knew it would be some time before we would see the band again. Little did we know, however, how much our lives were to change!

Two weeks later we were speechless; there was to be an addition to the family.

We saw the band many times up until Kevin was born. I remember phoning Dave to tell him about the pregnancy, saying "Snap" because I'd heard of Gilly's news. I took some time letting the band know about the birth, but I was surprised when Dave rang one day to ask us the news. In fact I was over the moon to think that he'd taken the trouble. We've missed quite a few gig since Kevin was born, but caught up in the Glasgow Pavilion in 1993. We took along pictures of Kevin and our ever-growing Blues Band photo album; they went down a treat.

So – here's to The Blues Band, and to many more gigs in the years to come!

PAT STIRLING

From Taunton, a brief but succinct view:

I know The Blues Band are not always at the top of the 'blues buffs' list. That's because they're popular, and the one thing you mustn't be in Britain is popular. Paul Jones has never been forgiven for becoming a 'luvvie'; but despite the unwarranted swipes by such serious 'critics', people who, frankly, have forgotten how to enjoy themselves, The Blues Band continue to deliver the goods. They rock, they roll, they play the blues and are still a unique combination of musicians who were the very roots of British pop. Showmen, gentlemen, and above all, Bluesmen. So what if P. J. is Uncle Jack? Has it affected his harp playing? No way.

GEORGE BREWER

There are hundreds of articulate fans whose glowing testimonies could be included here. Friends of the band in every way, just a few long-standing supporters deserve to be mentioned in dispatches; Wolfgang Pieker, Richard and Linda Austin, John Arkle, Sue Breese, Maureen Bell, Terry Charles, Eddie Clegg, Hazel Clifford, Carsten Drude, Jan Dicks, John and Pat Frankton, Val Fryer, Karen Foulkes, Michelle Galliers, Brenda Greenland, Werner Gabele, Lynda Gibson, Katie Howson, Munro Jack, Kathy Jones, Peter Kleeman, Jacky Kett, Peter Kleinsimon, Rob Loggie, Kim Laydon, Trevor Mann, Susan McEwan, Debbie and Mike Mohan, Brian Mills, Charmian Morgan, Vicki Newell, Peter Odgers, Sarah & Bill Oughton, Jamie Occomore, Jan Peters, Helen Page, Fran Page, Howie Palmer, Tim Price, Julian Purser, Anita Repo, Vanessa Ross and Tex, John Rigg, Sadie Roper, Jim Sadler, David A. Smith, Roger Stones, Wolfgang Schussler, Pat and John Standen, Angela Thim, K.M. Titcomb, Marc Van Der Gucht, Franz Verbeten, Terry Wigmore, Peter Wellman, Nic Walker, Susan Williams, Jason Wilkinson, Bob Wing, Luke Willis, Phil Windross, Terry Wigmore, Alan Walker....

These are people with a staggering commitment, just a selection of the many who have followed The Blues Band throughout their fifteen years. There are many others, obviously too numerous to acknowledge here, who discovered the band later. Few bands today have a more faithful and long-standing army of followers; in many ways this book is theirs, too.

Believe it or not this is Neil Stirling – the same boy featured at the chapter heading (the other bloke doesn't look much older though)

The Blues Band Recordings
1979 to 1994

To include all the various individual recording projects of individual band members would make for an interesting second volume to this work. Bob Hall, for instance, appears on over 85 albums; Paul Jones, apart from his Manfreds and solo works, has appeared on literally countless sessions over the last two decades, playing harmonica for just about every big name in pop. Tom McGuinness and Rob Townsend also have complex recording careers, and Dave Kelly's discography, (available in the Autumn 1990 issue of *Ready*, The Blues Band's newsletter) encompasses 25 years of work. Both Peter Filleul and Gary Fletcher have left a long trail of diverse work, and rather than flesh out this book with endless lists of material, much of which would be difficult or impossible to obtain, I list here The Blues Band's work to date.

ALBUMS

Official Blues Band Bootleg Album (Re-issued in 1991 by BMG 260497)	Blues Band BBBP 101	1979
Ready (Re-issued in 1991 by BMG 260410)	Arista 202887	1980
Itchy Feet (Re-issued in 1991 by BMG 260697)	Arista 203986	1981
Brand Loyalty (Re-issued in 1991 by BMG but now deleted)	Arista 204922	1982
Bye-Bye Blues (Re-issued in 1992 by Demon with extra tracks)	Arista 205256	1983
These Kind of Blues	Date DALP 4001160J	1986
Back for More (now deleted)	Ariola 210095 Cassette 410095 CD 260095	1989
Fat City	RCA/BMG PL75100 CD PD75100 Cassette PK75100	1991
Homage	Castle Communications CD ESSCD 202	1993

EXTENDED PLAY

Maggie's Farm/Ain't it Tough/ Diddy Wah Diddy/ Back Door Man	BOOT 2	1980

SINGLES

These singles are generally unavailable but were issued during the Band's time with Arista;

Come on In/The Blues Band Song	BOOT 1	1980
Find Yourself Another Fool/ SUS Blues	BOOT 3	1980
Nadine/That's All Right (two live tracks issued free with early copies of *Ready* album)	BLUES 1	1980
Who's Right, Who's Wrong/ Itchy Feet	BOOT 4	1981
Come On/Green Stuff	BOOT 5	1981
Take Me Home/So Bad	BOOT 6	1982
Hey Hey Little Girl/SUS Blues (issued free with BOOT 6 in a smart pink and orange gatefold sleeve; once these ran out BOOT 6 became an ordinary, lonely 45) A limited edition live single	BLUES 2	1982
Seemed Like a Good Idea/ Rolling Log	BOOT 7	1982
Blue Collar/Duisburg Blues (issued only as a promo for the *Back For More* album)	Ariola 113838	1989

According to Wolfgang Pieker in Germany there were three bootleg cassettes in general circulation in the 1980s; *Blues Band Live* at the Markthalle, Hamburg, 30.11.80, *Blues Band Live* at Ball Pompos, Kiel, 6.11.81 and *Dave Kelly Band Live* at The Fabrik, Hamburg, 1984. These are all forbidden fruit but the Hamburg one is really good.

For more information, why not subscribe to *Ready*, The Blues Band's quarterly newsletter. For five pounds sterling, you get the last four issues plus the next four, and answers to all your questions plus regular advance notices on upcoming gigs, TV and radio appearances, and buckets full of nostalgia. Write to: ROY BAINTON
13 West Hill Avenue
Mansfield
Nottinghamshire
NG18 1PQ, England.

When the best met the best: a break in recording at Nova Studios in the early 1980s. Ry Cooder's mighty backing vocalists joined forces to enhance a Dave Kelly session. Left to right: Gary, Willie Greene senior, Pico Payne, Dave, Bobby King and Lou Stonebridge. To hear the results of this collaboration, buy Making Whoopee *on the RPM label.*

*"The blues is based on somebody's life,
it hits 'em in the heart, and the love
comes out."*

Little Junior Parker